Determining
Faculty
Effectiveness

*Assessing Teaching, Research,
and Service For Personnel Decisions
and Improvement*

John A. Centra

Determining
Faculty
Effectiveness

Jossey-Bass Publishers
San Francisco • Washington • London • 1979

DETERMINING FACULTY EFFECTIVENESS
Assessing Teaching, Research, and Service
for Personnel Decisions and Improvement
        by John A. Centra

Copyright © 1979 by: Jossey-Bass Inc., Publishers
                        433 California Street
                        San Francisco, California 94104
                                  &
                        Jossey-Bass Limited
                        28 Banner Street
                        London EC1Y 8QE

Library of Congress Cataloging in Publication Data

Centra, John A
  Determining faculty effectiveness.

  Bibliography: p.
  Includes index.
  1. College teachers, Rating of. 2. Student
evaluation of teachers. I. Title.
LB2333.C45   378.1'2   79-88776
ISBN 0-87589-437-2

Manufactured in the United States of America

JACKET DESIGN BY WILLI BAUM

FIRST EDITION

Code 7935

*The Jossey-Bass Series
in Higher Education*

Preface

All too common are the stories about excellent teachers who fail to win promotions because they have not published, despite the fact that much of the publishing done by their colleagues is inconsequential; or about faculty members who get promoted by pleasing key people rather than by exceptional performance; or of professors who have not improved their teaching since leaving graduate school many years ago. I am not so naive as to think that *Determining Faculty Effectiveness* will do away with these or similar occurrences. But perhaps it will help.

My intention has been to make this book useful not only to teaching-improvement specialists and to administrators in charge of personnel decisions but also to faculty members who are having decisions made about them and who want to assess their own professional strengths and weaknesses. Thus, I provide many examples— of both evaluation forms and procedures. Rather than prescribing a specific system of assessment, however, I discuss general principles and guidelines and make suggestions for colleges to consider in developing their own approaches to evaluation. Because individuals should be involved in the development of an assessment system that affects them, and since circumstances often differ from one institution to another, each college should work out its own specific approach.

The suggestions and guidelines presented in this book rely heavily on research evidence and, in particular, my own studies over the past fifteen years. Research findings in the last few years have been especially illuminating in such areas as the use of student ratings, colleague evaluations, and self-assessment of instruction. In other areas the evidence is more limited, such as in the assessment and improvement of research productivity. It has been necessary to be selective in answering questions in these areas, but the questions addressed are ones that faculty members and administrators raise repeatedly at conferences, workshops, and seminars on faculty evaluation: I have tried to summarize the existing research evidence on these topics.

This book goes beyond earlier ones on faculty assessment in several ways. It not only includes recent research and approaches to assessment but also considers legal issues affecting faculty evaluation; for example, Title VII and other federal and state statutes requiring promotion practices to be job-related put a special burden on the criteria used and the procedures followed. The book equally emphasizes the dual and related purposes of assessment: improvement and decision making. And it discusses issues in the assessment of research and scholarship, public service, and advising that have not been addressed by other authors.

I would like to thank the Exxon Education Foundation, the Graduate Record Examinations Board, and, in particular, the Educational Testing Service for their support in carrying out several of the studies summarized in the book. I am grateful to the students and faculty members who participated in the studies. Over the years discussions and exchanges with my colleagues at the Educational Testing Service and with colleagues in the field have been especially helpful. And I thank Marian Helms, who converted my peculiar handwriting into the chapters that follow—not only with her exceptional typing skill but with typical good humor.

Princeton, New Jersey   JOHN A. CENTRA
October 1979

Contents

Contents

Assessing Teaching ● *Reviewing the Evidence* ● *The Review Process*

List of Exhibits

The Author

JOHN A. CENTRA is senior research psychologist at the Educational Testing Service in Princeton, New Jersey. He was awarded the B.A. degree in the social sciences from the State University of New York at Albany (1954), the M.A. degree in personnel psychology from Teachers College, Columbia University (1957), and the Ph.D. degree in education from Michigan State University (1965).

Centra has had administrative and research experience at Alfred University, State University College at Buffalo, and Michigan State University. He has also taught at New York University and has spent the past thirteen years in research at the Educational Testing Service. Among his publications are sixty articles and reports, almost half of which are devoted to studies and discussions of the assessment of teaching or the development of faculty members. He is the author of *Women, Men, and the Doctorate* (1974) and editor (and contributor) of *New Directions in Higher Education: Renewing and Evaluating College Teaching* (1977). Among his research monographs are

Strategies for Improving College Teaching (1972), *Faculty Development Practices in U.S. Colleges and Universities* (1976), *How Universities Evaluate Faculty Performance* (1977), and *College Enrollment in the 1980s: Projections and Possibilities* (1978). He is currently studying the research productivity patterns of faculty members.

Centra is a member of the American Psychological Association, the National Council on Measurement in Education, and the American Educational Research Association, for which he chairs the Instructional Evaluation special interest group. He has also participated in many conferences and workshops dealing with the assessment and improvement of faculty effectiveness.

To my wife, Nancy, and our daughters, Cathy, Liza, and Joan

Determining
Faculty
Effectiveness

*Assessing Teaching, Research,
and Service For Personnel Decisions
and Improvement*

ONE

Goals and Procedures of Faculty Evaluation

Faculty members are evaluated in order to decide whether they should be promoted or rewarded and to improve their performance—two purposes that need not be mutually exclusive. They should, in fact, go hand in hand. A faculty member's teaching, research, and other activities should be evaluated continuously to give that individual the opportunity to improve on weak points and build on strengths.

For many people, however, whether they are teachers or students, evaluation is a threat to their egos; others fear that the measures used will not or cannot rank them fairly. They are often right. Teachers do not always evaluate students properly and institutions frequently employ ill-defined and subjective means to assess faculty performance.

A number of faculty members resist evaluation of teaching, although most concede that some means must be found to prune the dead wood from their ranks. They base their resistance on two points:

1

the classroom is their personal realm and any attempt to assess what happens behind classroom doors is an invasion of their privacy; still others argue that how they teach and what they teach is their responsibility alone. They also question the efficacy of evaluating teaching methods, as evidenced by the following paragraph taken from a professor's letter to the *New York Times* (1977): "Unlike scholarship, which has a visible product, namely published reports, the results of teaching are locked in the heads of students and are usually not apparent, even to the students themselves, for a very long time." Those long-term effects on students are difficult to measure and even more difficult to attribute to a specific course or teacher. But it does not follow that teaching cannot be evaluated. It can and is being appraised—although, as with the assessment of scholarly attainment, not always perfectly.

In the past, particularly during the expansion years of the 1960s, colleges could get by with poorly defined evaluation procedures. Many colleges were concerned largely with recruiting and keeping competent faculty members. Tenure and promotion were almost automatic unless a faculty member was obviously incompetent. But enrollments have tapered off in recent years, and colleges no longer need to add staff members. College budgets are tight and many institutions are at or near prescribed limits in the percentage of faculty on tenure (62 percent of all faculty members had tenure in 1977 [AAUP, 1978]). Teachers must now prove that they deserve tenure, forcing institutions to make fine distinctions between generally competent instructors.

The declining rate of growth has also resulted in less faculty mobility. Colleges can no longer depend on new staff to keep them vital, nor can teachers broaden perspectives by changing jobs. This steady-state condition is being remedied, in part, by teacher evaluation and improvement programs. Additional pressure to upgrade instruction comes from students, parents, and legislators. Students seem less timid in expressing dissatisfaction than they once were, and many parents are not at all sure that the effectiveness of instruction warrants the high costs of a college education. Legislators are pressuring public institutions to become more accountable and in a few instances have legislated evaluation requirements; in states such as California they have earmarked funds specifically for instructional improvement.

Institutions are increasingly faced with litigation and with court rulings on such fundamental issues as the adequacy of courses offered and the rights of teachers in dismissal cases. Consider, for example, the complaint by students that a course had little substance, did not match the catalogue description, and lacked adequate evaluation of student performance. These were the exact charges brought by a student in the case of *Ianello* v. *The University of Bridgeport*, eventually dismissed by the court only because the student failed to prove her case. The courts do not seem reluctant to rule against an institution. A Tennessee court, in the case of *Lowenthal* v. *Vanderbilt University*, ruled that a doctoral program in management was inadequate; thus judges clearly feel they have the expertise to decide academic matters (Carnegie Council on Policy Studies in Higher Education, 1979). The classroom is no longer the sole domain of the teacher. Students also have rights, and colleges have a responsibility to ensure the quality of courses and programs offered.

The increase in litigation—and its threat—have increased the formality of faculty evaluation. More frequently, procedures are spelled out and evaluation summaries are written and placed in personnel folders. Due process must be demonstrated in the event of contested decisions. The relaxed atmosphere of past decades is seldom found.

In spite of the problems, reasons for effective evaluation are becoming increasingly compelling. Of the many sources of information that might be used to evaluate teaching and research, only a few are used or usable. To better understand and apply the methods now available, they will be examined more closely in the following chapters. Evaluating teaching, because it is particularly elusive, will receive special attention. In discussing the major approaches—student ratings, colleague input, self-evaluations, and evidence of how well students have learned—the emphasis will be on research studies.

There is no single foolproof way to evaluate teaching. Each source of information or approach has its limitations; each can be biased or contaminated. Fair personnel decisions can best be made by combining information from several sources so that the shortcomings of one approach can be balanced by the strengths of another. This system of checks and balances is particularly crucial in making tenure, promotion, or salary decisions; it is also useful in maximizing the results of evaluation for instructional improvement. What works with some teachers may not be effective for all.

What Evaluation Practices Are Currently Used?

In 1976, 453 department heads at 134 colleges and universities responded to a request for their methods used to evaluate faculty for promotion, salary increases, or tenure (Centra, 1977a). The survey results in general indicate that, once the appropriate credentials are in hand, most such institutions evaluate faculty members as research scholars and classroom teachers, the emphasis varying according to the level and goals of the institutions or the department. Serving on dissertation committees and supervising student research, both considered part of one's teaching responsibility in universities, are also considered. The majority of two-year colleges, liberal arts colleges, and masters-level institutions place major importance on the quality of teaching performance, a finding also indicated by other surveys (Seldin, 1978; Astin and Lee, 1967). In addition, these institutions seem to put more emphasis on advising than do those with doctoral programs (Boyd and Schietinger, 1976).

The questionnaire included thirteen general criteria that might be used in evaluating individual faculty members (see Exhibit 1). Replies are grouped according to an institutional classification scheme developed by the Carnegie Commission on Higher Education (1973), and includes Research Universities (the 100 to 150 institutions that lead in federal financial support or doctorates awarded), Doctoral-Granting Universities (those that attract less financial support or award fewer degrees than Research Universities), and Comprehensive Universities and Colleges (those offering liberal arts plus professional or occupational programs). Classroom teaching, quality of publications, and personal qualifications (academic degrees and professional experience) are most frequently reported as major or extremely critical factors in judging faculty members. As indicated in Exhibit 1, however, department heads in the three different types of institutions give different emphasis to each of the three criteria. Less weight is placed on classroom teaching and personal qualifications at Research Universities than at Doctoral-Granting Universities and Comprehensive Universities and Colleges. Since there may be little

Exhibit 1. Average Weight Given to Various Criteria for Evaluating Total Faculty Performance, by University Level

Criteria

Classroom teaching

Quality of publications

Number of publications

Personal qualifications (academic degrees, professional experience, and so on)

Research and/or creative activity (independent of publication)

Supervision of student research, including serving on master's and doctoral committees

Campus committee work, service to college

Activity in professional societies (hold office, edit journal, and so on)

Student advising

Personality factors

Public or community service

Competing job offers

Consultation (government, business, and so on)

Not a Factor

Minor Factor

Major Factor

Extremely Critical Factor

Key:

Research Universities

Doctoral-Granting Universities

Comprehensive Universities and Colleges

variation in personal qualifications among candidates for tenure in Research Universities, having an advanced degree and appropriate experience receives less weighting at those institutions. Not surprisingly, the quality of publications is judged as more important by department heads in Research Universities than by those at either of the other two university levels. Department heads in Comprehensive Universities and Colleges give quality of publications essentially the same weight as number of publications or college service (such as campus committee work).

Department heads are not entirely satisfied with the relative emphasis given to these criteria. They prefer to place more emphasis on the quality of publications and less on the number of publications; they also would like to see student advising and the supervision of student research given more weight. Several criteria are not considered important in evaluating faculty, and most department heads think they should not be; these include competing job offers, consultation, public or community service, and personality characteristics.

The lack of importance given to public or community service is somewhat surprising. Other surveys find, however, that a small number of institutions (10 percent or so) give public or community service as much weight in promotion decisions as they give to teaching and research (McCarthy, 1978; Boyd and Schietinger, 1976). Generally more important is campus committee work and service to the institution (see Exhibit 1); indeed, some observers argue that serving on influential committees and getting along with colleagues are exceeded in importance only by teaching and research performance (Nitzsche, 1978).

Whether teaching does in fact receive as much weight in promotion and tenure decisions as suggested by the results in Exhibit 1 or whether department heads are merely paying lip service to its importance is difficult to know. Faculty in the Oregon State University system consider publications to be the most influential evidence in decisions on advancement (Thorne, Scott, and Beaird, 1976). And some institutions appear to be emphasizing scholarly achievement more than ever. A 1977 story in the *Chronicle of Higher Education*, for example, told of an assistant professor, apparently an effective teacher, who was denied tenure because of his lack of published research

(Weeks, 1977). In its efforts to become "a really first-rate university," according to the provost, this institution raised promotion and tenure standards so that they "were more rigorous now than at any time in the institution's history and comparable with many of the outstanding schools in the country." This is probably not an isolated instance. Given the increasing number of Ph.D.s looking for academic jobs, universities trying to establish national reputations are more selective regarding scholarly activity and publications. Good teaching by itself has increasingly become a necessary but not a sufficient reason for promotion.

How Is Teaching Evaluated? Increasingly, it appears that evaluation of teaching is based on systematic student ratings and on the content of course syllabi and examinations. Department chairmen rank fifteen possible sources of information according to their importance in teacher assessment, listing as most influential chairman evaluations, systematic student ratings, and colleagues' opinions; least used are videotapes of classroom teaching, the long-term follow-up of students, alumni ratings, colleague ratings based on classroom visits, and student examination performance (Centra, 1977a).

Exhibit 2 ranks the sources of information according to current importance and the importance each should have. Many department heads would prefer to increase the weight of student ratings and lessen that of colleagues' opinions, but they would like to place more emphasis on colleague ratings based on classroom visits, currently not a factor in many departments. Other research (see Chapter Four) shows that in most instances colleague ratings based on classroom observation are not sufficiently reliable; they require more time spent in visitations or training sessions.

Department heads also believe that the content of course syllabi and examinations should be given more importance in evaluations, and they would like to emphasize a long-term follow-up of student performance. Unfortunately, as pointed out earlier, the assessment of student learning years after completion of a course, while possibly an ideal indicator of the long-term effects of a course or a teacher, is a difficult measure to obtain in any systematic and usable way. An assessment of end-of-course learning, although more manageable, is also subject to misinterpretation when used in tenure and promotion

Exhibit 2. Ranking for Current and Preferred Sources of Information for Evaluating Teaching Performance, by Carnegie Institutional Classification

	Current Use and Importance				Importance Each Should Have			
	All N=453	I N=158	II N=122	III N=173	All	I	II	III
Chairman evaluation	1	3	1	1	2	2	2	1
Colleagues' opinions	2.5	1	3	2	3	3	3	4
Systematic student ratings	2.5	2	2	4	1	1	1	2
Committee evaluation	4	4	4	3	4	4	4	3
Informal student opinions	5	5	5	6	6	6	7	7.5
Dean evaluation	6	8	6	5	8	11	9	6
Content of course syllabi and examinations	7	7	8	7	5	5	5	5
Popularity of elective courses (for example, enrollment)	8	6	7	10	13	10	14	13
Self-evaluation or report	9	10	9	8.5	11	14	10	10
Teaching improvement activities (participation in workshops, in-service programs, and so on)	10	11	11	8.5	10	12.5	11	7.5
Student examination performance	11	9	12	11	12	9	13	12
Colleague ratings based on classroom visits	12	12	10	12	7	7	6	9
Alumni opinions or ratings	13	13	13	14	14	12.5	12	14
Long-term follow up of how students perform	14	14	14	13	9	8	8	11
Videotape of classroom teaching	15	15	15	15	15	15	15	15

Note: Departments grouped by university classification as follows: I=Research Universities; II=Doctoral-Granting Universities; III=Comprehensive Universities and Colleges.

decisions. No doubt, however, student learning is an important criterion in assessing teaching, and could be considered under the right circumstances.

In comparison to surveys of evaluation practices in the 1960s (Astin and Lee, 1967), colleges and universities are currently relying more on systematic student ratings and, to some extent, on the content of course syllabi and examinations. However, informal student opinions have been supplanted by formal student rating questionnaires and procedures which, in most instances, can provide a more reliable assessment of student views. It is noteworthy that student ratings are more important in Research and Doctoral-Granting Universities than in Comprehensive Universities and Colleges.

Yet in the latter group and among liberal arts colleges, the increase in the use of student ratings to evaluate teaching performance has been extraordinary. Seldin (1978) surveyed academic deans at over 400 colleges in 1973 and again in 1978. He found that 53 percent "always used" systematic student ratings to evaluate teaching in 1978, compared to 29 percent in 1973. The use of course syllabi and examinations jumped from about 10 to 14 percent of the institutions in the five-year span, and self-evaluation from 20 to 36 percent.

Although student ratings are being increasingly used to assess teaching for administrative purposes, the most important person consulted in almost all types of institutions is the department chairman. Committee evaluation and academic deans (especially among the smaller institutions) are also critical, though from all indications these groups are placing more emphasis on systematic student ratings and whatever objective information can be provided in a faculty member's dossier.

While there have not been any recent national surveys of how two-year colleges evaluate teaching for decisions on advancement, they seem to use student ratings at least as much as at other types of institutions. In the mid 1960s, an estimated 16 percent of the two-year colleges and 11 percent of the liberal arts colleges reported using systematic student ratings in all or most departments (Astin and Lee, 1967). Over half of the liberal arts colleges now use student ratings extensively, as is probably the case with two-year colleges as well. Many two-year colleges emphasize behavioral objectives or mastery learning approaches and evaluate teachers on how well they adopt these methods (see, for example, Boyd and Schietinger, 1976; Moomaw, 1977). A few of these colleges go a step further and evaluate faculty members according to the number of students who achieve a specified level of competence in a course.

How Do Colleges Assess Teaching for Instructional Improvement? Colleges are using a variety of ways to analyze shortcomings in teaching and courses. The information is often gathered as part of a faculty development or instructional development program. In a 1976 survey of faculty development practices at 756 campuses throughout the country (Centra, 1976a), colleges report the use of assessment techniques as one of four major approaches to improve teaching. The others are "traditional" practices such as temporary teaching-load reductions, annual awards in teaching, and sabbatical leaves (these are most often found at larger colleges and universities); "instructional assistance" practices, featuring specialists to assist faculty in instructional development, in the use of audiovisual aids, or in instructional technology (found generally at larger two-year colleges and universities with faculty development units); "high faculty involvement" practices, or those that tend to involve a high proportion of the faculty since they are run both for and by faculty members (for example, senior faculty work with inexperienced teachers).

An analysis or an assessment of teaching might come from students, from colleagues, from experts, by use of videotape, or by other means. Ideally, the practices provide the teacher—or possibly a development specialist—with the kind of diagnostic information that can be used to modify and improve what a teacher does. The survey questionnaire listed ten ways of evaluating or analyzing teachers. Estimates of their use and effectiveness, usually provided by a faculty development person or an administrator at each college, are given in Exhibit 3. While the responses presumably reflect the use of practices for instructional improvement, evaluations in some instances are probably used in personnel decisions. It is not always possible to separate the two purposes. Student ratings, for example, may be voluntarily submitted by a teacher as evidence of teaching effectiveness even though the ratings are collected largely for instructional improvement.

Systematic student ratings to help faculty improve instruction are used by at least a fifth of the faculty at over 80 percent of the 756 institutions and are reported to be moderately effective by about half of the respondents (fewer university than two- or four-year college respondents see them as effective). Formal or informal assessments by colleagues are less effective than consulting with experienced faculty or working with master teachers (see numbers 4 and 5 versus 7 and 8 in Exhibit 3). The analysis of in-class videotapes to improve instruction is one of the more effective practices, though it is used by only a very small proportion of the faculty on campuses where it is available (about 60 percent of the institutions). Another practice rated effective but little used is the professional and personal development plan for individual faculty members (practice number 6): just under 40 percent of the institutions use this practice with at least 5 percent of their faculty, and almost two thirds of the respondents from these colleges rate it as effective. These individual development plans, known also as growth contracts, usually call for a self-development program to be drawn up by a faculty member in conjunction with a development specialist or administrator. The growth contract and the use of in-class videotapes will be discussed more fully in Chapter Three.

Generally speaking, the analysis or assessment practices are rated as more effective by respondents from two-year colleges than by those from either four-year colleges or universities. For example, 55 percent of the two-year college respondents rate formal assessments by colleagues as effective, compared to 42 percent of the respondents from four-year colleges and 33 percent of those from the universities. More faculty members at the two-year colleges use such practices as assessments by colleagues or administrators and growth contracts. Since universities and some four-year colleges emphasize research as well as teaching, we might expect that a smaller number of faculty members at these institutions are interested in analyzing their teaching or in employing other practices to improve classroom instruction.

How Are Scholarship and Research Currently Evaluated? Only a minority of faculty members publish or carry on research in any substantial sense. The 1977 survey of the American professoriate by Ladd and Lipset, for example, found that 29 percent had never published an article and 60 percent had never published more than four articles. Based on a random sample of 4,300 faculty members

Exhibit 3. Estimated Use and Effectiveness of Analysis or Assessment Practices, by Type of Institution

Two-Year Colleges, N=326
Four-Year Colleges, N=315
Universities, N=93

Analysis or Assessment Practices	Type of Inst.	Estimated Extent of Faculty Use in Percentages[a]					Estimated Effectiveness[b] Percentage Indicating Effective or Very Effective
		Not Used	Fewer than 5	5-20	20-50	Over 50	
1. Systematic ratings of instruction by students used to help faculty improve	2-yr	4	6	10	13	67	58
	4-yr	3	3	9	16	69	46
	univ.	1	4	14	12	69	32
2. Systematic teaching or course evaluations by an administrator for improvement purposes	2-yr	19	7	10	15	48	60
	4-yr	46	9	12	5	24	45
	univ.	41	23	15	3	16	41
3. System for faculty to assess their own strengths and areas needing improvement	2-yr	24	9	12	12	40	61
	4-yr	39	11	13	10	25	53
	univ.	38	21	18	8	16	53

4. Formal assessments by colleagues for teaching or course improvement (that is, visitations or use of assessment form)	2-yr	34	14	11	13	27	55
	4-yr	38	21	13	8	18	42
	univ.	23	32	24	13	8	33
5. Informal assessments by colleagues for teaching or course improvement	2-yr	30	18	19	16	14	47
	4-yr	20	19	26	19	12	39
	univ.	11	32	28	18	10	24
6. Professional and personal development plan (sometimes called a growth contract) for individual faculty members	2-yr	55	7	7	5	23	71
	4-yr	69	12	8	3	5	56
	univ.	68	17	7	2	3	44
7. Faculty with expertise consult with other faculty on teaching or course improvement	2-yr	28	25	24	13	8	64
	4-yr	33	27	22	13	3	57
	univ.	27	44	19	10	0	61
8. "Master teachers" or senior faculty work closely with new or apprentice teachers	2-yr	47	18	18	7	8	62
	4-yr	62	19	8	6	3	56
	univ.	51	29	16	2	1	52
9. Classroom visitation by an instructional resource person (that is, a development specialist), upon request, followed by a diagnosis of teaching	2-yr	59	19	11	4	5	56
	4-yr	71	19	5	1	1	53
	univ.	42	52	5	1	0	37
10. Analysis of in-class videotapes to improve instruction	2-yr	42	33	16	4	2	66
	4-yr	45	35	14	3	1	54
	univ.	27	61	10	0	1	54

[a] For each item the "no response" rate was between 1 and 3 percent.
[b] Percentages based only on institutions at which practice existed.

from 158 institutions, their survey showed further that 59 percent had never written or edited a book or monograph and 60 percent had never received funding for research. The advancement-of-knowledge function, no doubt a crucial purpose of higher education, thus is carried out by fewer than half of all college professors, and a relatively small portion of these seem to contribute truly significant work in their fields.

Some indications of how colleges and universities evaluate research and scholarship are provided in the survey of department heads at 134 institutions (Centra, 1977a). Out of sixteen criteria, the three given the most weight are the number of articles published in quality journals, the number of books published (as sole or senior author), and the quality of research as judged by peers at the institution. The number of citations of one's work, unpublished papers or reports, and self-evaluations receive only minor consideration. Other types of information, such as research grants or professional awards received, vary in importance. The sixteen criteria are rank-ordered in Exhibit 4 for the three levels of institutions. Research Universities tend to emphasize more the judgment of peers—both from within and without the institution—than do either Doctoral-Granting Universities or Comprehensive Universities and Colleges. Comprehensive Universities and Colleges, in fact, emphasize least most of the criteria listed, since research and scholarship are generally less important at these institutions.

The evaluation of research and scholarship generally depends very much on the type of department and the level of institution. The number of books and papers produced, for example, is especially important in humanities departments at two levels of universities, but not at the third (Comprehensive Universities and Colleges). Peer judgments of research and the number of articles in quality journals are more important in social science departments at Research Universities than at Comprehensive Universities and Colleges. Natural science departments, regardless of type of institution, emphasize grants or funding received much more than do other departments.

Most department heads in Research Universities are satisfied with the way in which they evaluate scholarship or research and see no need for major changes, while department heads in Doctoral Universities and in Comprehensive Universities and Colleges prefer

Exhibit 4. Ranking for Current and Preferred Criteria for Evaluating Research or Scholarship Performance, by Carnegie Institutional Classification

	Current Use and Importance				Importance Each Should Have			
	All N=453	I N=158	II N=122	III N=173	All	I	II	III
Number of:								
Articles in *quality* journals	1	1	1	3	1	1	1	1
Books as sole or senior author	2	3	2	1	2	4	2	2
Publications in all professional journals	4	5	6.5	2	7	7	11	7
Monographs or chapters in books	6	7	5	7.5	6	6	6	6
Books as junior author or editor	10	9	11	9	9	10	9	8
Papers at professional meetings	11	11	13	7.5	11	9	12	9
Unpublished papers or reports	14	15	4	14	15	15	15	13
Citations of published materials	15	13	15	15.5	13	13	14	14
Quality of scholarly research and publications as judged by:								
Peers at the institution	3	2	3	4	3	2	3	3
Peers at other institutions	7	4	9	12	4	3	4	5
Department chairman	8.5	8	8	10	8	8	7	12
Dean	13	14	14	13	14	14	13	15
Self-evaluations	16	16	16	15.5	16	16	16	16
Grants for funding received	8.5	10	10	6	10	11	8	10
Referee or editor of professional journal	12	12	12	11	12	12	10	11
Honors or awards from profession	5	6	6.5	5	5	5	5	4

Note: Departments grouped by university classification as follows: I=Research Universities; II=Doctoral-Granting Universities; III=Comprehensive Universities and Colleges.

to give more importance to peer judgments at other institutions and less importance to the sheer number of articles in all types of journals.

Overview

In the remaining chapters the evaluation of faculty performance will be discussed as it relates to using the collected information to make personnel decisions or to improve faculty performance in their various activities. Evaluators refer to the former as *summative evaluation* because it "sums up" performance at the end of a time period and results in some kind of overall judgment. Evaluation to improve performance can be called *formative* because it is meant to help "form" performance while it is in progress. Chapters Two through Five discuss the evaluation of teaching—the strengths and limitations of student ratings (Chapter Two), self-assessment and self-analysis, which includes audio and video playback as well as the so-called individualized development plan (Chapter Three), colleague evaluations (Chapter Four), and the assessment of student learning (Chapter Five). Chapter Six considers the evaluation of research, advising, and public service, and Chapter Seven discusses legal concerns in personnel policy. Key questions are raised in each of the chapters, research related to each of these questions is summarized, and recommendations are offered at the chapter's conclusion.

The final chapter summarizes some key points and details a comprehensive model of faculty evaluation with reference to other models. It also discusses the administrator's role and methods of using evaluation information for personnel decisions.

TWO

Uses and Limitations
of Student Ratings

Despite some strong opposition
to incorporating student ratings in faculty evaluation, they are widely
used and endorsed by both students and faculty members. Seventy-two
percent of responding college freshmen in the 1977 annual survey by
the American Council on Education (ACE) felt that they should help
to evaluate faculty performance (Astin, 1978). The past half dozen
ACE surveys reported similar findings. And in 1972 nearly 70 percent
of a national sample of faculty members agreed that "faculty
promotions should be based in part on formal student evaluations of
their teaching" (Bayer, 1973).

Student ratings take place at the end of the course and are
generally described as informal or formal. Informal student evaluations involve occasional comments to the instructor or the dean by a
few students in the class. Such opinions may not represent the views
of all the students and are therefore less useful than those comprehensive or formal systems that ask students for written responses to a set of

short-answer, open-ended questions concerning the course and the teaching methods.

What Are the Characteristics of Effective Teaching?

Many techniques have been used over the years to identify potentially useful items for inclusion in formal systems of rating teaching and courses. A widely used method requests the opinions of faculty members, students, administrators, and alumni. Using such consultation, a University of Toledo study (Perry and Baumann, 1973) identified some sixty teacher behaviors that students, faculty, and alumni associated with effective teaching. Ranked high in teaching value by all three groups were such behaviors as being well prepared for class and exhibiting interest in the subject under study, while items with low teaching value included being neatly dressed or having irritating personal mannerisms.

Hildebrand, Wilson, and Dienst (1971) sought to describe effective teaching by a survey of students and faculty at the University of California, Davis. Students—asked to identify the best and the worst teachers that they had had in the previous year and to describe their teaching—included as distinguishing features of good teaching such items as "explains clearly, . . . seems to enjoy teaching, . . . makes difficult topics easy to understand, . . . knows if class is understanding the teacher or not, . . . keeps well informed about class progress, . . . is sensitive to student's desire to ask a question." Faculty members queried in the same survey listed such comments on good teaching by their colleagues as "seems to have a congenial relationship with students, . . . uses well-chosen examples to clarify points, . . . emphasizes *ways* of solving problems rather than solutions, . . . is an excellent public speaker" (emphasis added).

In 1975, Wotruba and Wright summarized twenty-one studies in which various groups had been asked to identify the qualities of effective teaching. The resulting list, typical of what would be found in most studies of this kind, included ten most frequently named characteristics:

- Communication skills—clearly interprets abstract ideas and theories
- Favorable attitudes toward students

- Knowledge of subject
- Good organization of subject matter and course
- Enthusiasm about subject
- Fairness in examinations and grading
- Willingness to experiment—flexible
- Encouragement of students to think for themselves
- Interesting lecturer—good speaking ability

Studies such as these have generated a pool of items that institutions can use in developing the hundreds of rating forms that have been developed over the years. (The best-known of these instruments are briefly described in the Appendix.) Two commercial forms currently used by the largest number of colleges are the Educational Testing Service's (ETS) Student Instructional Report (SIR) and the Instructional Development and Effectiveness Assessment System (IDEA) from Kansas State University (see Exhibits 5 and 6).

What Should Be the Content of Rating Forms?

Factor analysis studies of student ratings published over the past twenty-five years (examples are Coffman, 1954; Hodgson, 1958; Isaacson and others, 1964; Centra, 1973a) have identified several common dimensions or groups of items. Three of those appearing in the majority of instruments devised are (1) organization, structure, or clarity, (2) teacher-student interaction or rapport, and (3) teaching skill, communication, or lecturing ability (see Exhibit 7). Other categories included occasionally in rating instruments are evaluations of the course workload or difficulty, grading and examinations, impact on students (self-rated student accomplishment), and global or overall effectiveness.

Teachers can add five to ten optional items to most machine-scored forms in order to obtain student reactions to such areas as particular assignments, tests, and techniques used. With optional items, students can also rate the achievement of specific course objectives. Grasha (1977) describes one such procedure. The instructor, after reviewing each objective, asks students to identify any objective that has not been made clear during the course and to explain the reasons for this lack of clarity. Students are asked to indicate their difficulties in achieving each objective and to name the factors re-

Exhibit 5. Student Instructional Report

This questionnaire gives you an opportunity to express anonymously your views of this course and the way it has been taught. Indicate the response closest to your view by blackening the appropriate oval. Use a soft lead pencil (preferably No. 2) for all responses to the questionnaire. Do not use an ink or ball point pen.

SIR Report Number

SECTION I Items 1-20. Blacken one response number for each question.

NA (0) = Not Applicable or don't know. The statement does not apply to this course or instructor, or you simply are not able to give a knowledgeable response.

SA (4) = Strongly Agree. You strongly agree with the statement as it applies to this course or instructor.

A (3) = Agree. You agree more than you disagree with the statement as it applies to this course or instructor.

D (2) = Disagree. You disagree more than you agree with the statement as it applies to this course or instructor.

SD (1) = Strongly Disagree. You strongly disagree with the statement as it applies to this course or instructor.

		NA	SA	A	D	SD
1.	The instructor's objectives for the course have been made clear............	⓪	④	③	②	①
2.	There was considerable agreement between the announced objectives of the course and what was actually taught.........	⓪	④	③	②	①
3.	The instructor used class time well..........	⓪	④	③	②	①
4.	The instructor was readily available for consultation with students.........	⓪	④	③	②	①
5.	The instructor seemed to know when students didn't understand the material........	⓪	④	③	②	①
6.	Lectures were too repetitive of what was in the textbook(s).........	⓪	④	③	②	①
7.	The instructor encouraged students to think for themselves.........	⓪	④	③	②	①
8.	The instructor seemed genuinely concerned with students' progress and was actively helpful.........	⓪	④	③	②	①
9.	The instructor made helpful comments on papers or exams.........	⓪	④	③	②	①
10.	The instructor raised challenging questions or problems for discussion.........	⓪	④	③	②	①
11.	In this class I felt free to ask questions or express my opinions.........	⓪	④	③	②	①
12.	The instructor was well-prepared for each class.........	⓪	④	③	②	①
13.	The instructor told students how they would be evaluated in the course.........	⓪	④	③	②	①
14.	The instructor summarized or emphasized major points in lectures or discussions.........	⓪	④	③	②	①
15.	My interest in the subject area has been stimulated by this course.........	⓪	④	③	②	①
16.	The scope of the course has been too limited; not enough material has been covered.........	⓪	④	③	②	①
17.	Examinations reflected the important aspects of the course.........	⓪	④	③	②	①
18.	I have been putting a good deal of effort into this course.........	⓪	④	③	②	①
19.	The instructor was open to other viewpoints.........	⓪	④	③	②	①
20.	In my opinion, the instructor has accomplished (is accomplishing) his or her objectives for the course.........	⓪	④	③	②	①

SECTION II Items 21-31. Blacken one response number for each question.

21. For my preparation and ability, the level of difficulty of this course was:

  ① Very elementary   ④ Somewhat difficult
  ② Somewhat elementary   ⑤ Very difficult
  ③ About right

22. The work load for this course in relation to other courses of equal credit was:

  ① Much lighter   ④ Heavier
  ② Lighter   ⑤ Much heavier
  ③ About the same

23. For me, the pace at which the instructor covered the material during the term was:

  ① Very slow   ④ Somewhat fast
  ② Somewhat slow   ⑤ Very fast
  ③ Just about right

24. To what extent did the instructor use examples or illustrations to help clarify the material?

  ④ Frequently   ② Seldom
  ③ Occasionally   ① Never

Questionnaire continued on the other side.

572MRC116P200X
283562

Exhibit 5. (continued)

25. Was class size satisfactory for the method of conducting the class?

① Yes, most of the time ③ No, class was too small
② No, class was too large ④ It didn't make any differ- ence one way or the other

26. Which one of the following best describes this course for you?

① Major requirement or elective within major field
② Minor requirement or required elective out- side major field
③ College requirement but not part of my major or minor field
④ Elective not required in any way
⑤ Other

27. Which one of the following was your most important reason for selecting this course?

① Friend(s) recommended it
② Faculty advisor's recommendation
③ Teacher's excellent reputation
④ Thought I could make a good grade
⑤ Could use pass/no credit option
⑥ It was required
⑦ Subject was of interest
⑧ Other

28. What grade do you expect to receive in this course?

1 A 5 Fail
2 B 6 Pass
3 C 7 No credit
4 D 8 Other

29. What is your approximate cumulative grade-point average?

1 3.50-4.00 6 1.00-1.49
2 3.00-3.49 7 Less than 1.00
3 2.50-2.99 8 None yet
4 2.00-2.49
5 1.50-1.99

30. What is your class level?

1 Freshman 4 Senior
2 Sophomore 5 Graduate
3 Junior 6 Other

31. Sex:

1 Female
2 Male

SECTION III Items 32-39. Blacken one response number for each question.

Not applicable, don't know, or there were none. / Excellent / Good / Satisfactory / Fair / Poor

		NA	Excellent	Good	Satisfactory	Fair	Poor
32.	Overall, I would rate the textbook(s)	0	⑤	④	③	②	①
33.	Overall, I would rate the supplementary readings	0	⑤	④	③	②	①
34.	Overall, I would rate the quality of the exams	0	⑤	④	③	②	①
35.	I would rate the general quality of the lectures	0	⑤	④	③	②	①
36.	I would rate the overall value of class discussions	0	⑤	④	③	②	①
37.	Overall, I would rate the laboratories	0	⑤	④	③	②	①
38.	I would rate the overall value of this course to me as	0	⑤	④	③	②	①

39. Compared to other instructors you have had (secondary school and college), how effective has the instructor been in this course? (Blacken one response number.)

One of the most effective (among the top 10%)	More effective than most (among the top 30%)	About average	Not as effective as most (in the lowest 30%)	One of the least effective (in the lowest 10%)
⑤	④	③	②	①

SECTION IV Items 40-49. If the instructor provided supplementary questions and response options, use this section for responding. Blacken only one response number for each question.

	NA												NA									
40.	⓪	①	②	③	④	⑤	⑥	⑦	⑧	⑨		45.	⓪	①	②	③	④	⑤	⑥	⑦	⑧	⑨
41.	⓪	①	②	③	④	⑤	⑥	⑦	⑧	⑨		46.	⓪	①	②	③	④	⑤	⑥	⑦	⑧	⑨
42.	⓪	①	②	③	④	⑤	⑥	⑦	⑧	⑨		47.	⓪	①	②	③	④	⑤	⑥	⑦	⑧	⑨
43.	⓪	①	②	③	④	⑤	⑥	⑦	⑧	⑨		48.	⓪	①	②	③	④	⑤	⑥	⑦	⑧	⑨
44.	⓪	①	②	③	④	⑤	⑥	⑦	⑧	⑨		49.	⓪	①	②	③	④	⑤	⑥	⑦	⑧	⑨

If you would like to make additional comments about the course or instruction, use a separate sheet of paper. You might elaborate on the particular aspects you liked most as well as those you liked least. Also, how can the course or the way it was taught be improved? PLEASE GIVE THESE COMMENTS TO THE INSTRUCTOR.

If you have any comments or suggestions about this questionnaire (for example, the content or responses available), please send them to: Student Instructional Report, Educational Testing Service, Princeton, New Jersey 08540.

Exhibit 6. Instructional Development and Effectiveness
Assessment System (IDEA)

 SURVEY FORM -- STUDENT REACTIONS TO INSTRUCTION AND COURSES

Your thoughtful answers to these questions will provide helpful information to your instructor.

● Describe the frequency of your instructor's teaching procedures, using the following code:
1 — Hardly Ever   3 — Sometimes
2 — Occasionally   4 — Frequently   5 — Almost Always

The Instructor:

1. Promoted teacher-student discussion (as opposed to mere responses to questions).
2. Found ways to help students answer their own questions.
3. Encouraged students to express themselves freely and openly.
4. Seemed enthusiastic about the subject matter.
5. Changed approaches to meet new situations.
6. Gave examinations which stressed unnecessary memorization.
7. Spoke with expressiveness and variety in tone of voice.
8. Demonstrated the importance and significance of the subject matter.
9. Made presentations which were dry and dull.
10. Made it clear how each topic fit into the course.
11. Explained the reasons for criticisms of students' academic performance.
12. Gave examination questions which were unclear.
13. Encouraged student comments even when they turned out to be incorrect or irrelevant.
14. Summarized material in a manner which aided retention.
15. Stimulated students to intellectual effort beyond that required by most courses.
16. Clearly stated the objectives of the course.
17. Explained course material clearly, and explanations were to the point.
18. Related course material to real life situations.
19. Gave examination questions which were unreasonably detailed (picky).
20. Introduced stimulating ideas about the subject.

● On each of the objectives listed below, rate the progress you have made in this course compared with that made in other courses you have taken at this college or university. In this course my progress was:
1 — Low (lowest 10 per cent of courses I have taken here)
2 — Low Average (next 20 per cent of courses)
3 — Average (middle 40 per cent of courses)
4 — High Average (next 20 percent of courses)
5 — High (highest 10 per cent of courses)

Progress on:

21. Gaining factual knowledge (terminology, classifications, methods, trends).
22. Learning fundamental principles, generalizations, or theories.
23. Learning to apply course material to improve rational thinking, problem-solving and decision making.
24. Developing specific skills, competencies, and points of view needed by professionals in the field most closely related to this course.
25. Learning how professionals in this field go about the process of gaining new knowledge.
26. Developing creative capacities.
27. Developing a sense of personal responsibility (self-reliance, self-discipline).
28. Gaining a broader understanding and appreciation of intellectual-cultural activity (music, science, literature, etc.).
29. Developing skill in expressing myself orally or in writing.
30. Discovering the implications of the course material for understanding myself (interests, talents, values, etc.).

● On the next four questions, compare this course with others you have taken at this institution, using the following code:
1 — Much Less than Most Courses
2 — Less than Most
3 — About Average
4 — More than Most
5 — Much More than Most

The Course:

31. Amount of reading
32. Amount of work in other (non-reading) assignments
33. Difficulty of subject matter
34. Degree to which the course hung together (various topics and class activities were related to each other)

● Describe your attitudes toward and behavior in this course, using the following code:
1 — Definitely False
2 — More False than True   4 — More True than False
3 — In Between   5 — Definitely True

Self-rating:

35. I worked harder on this course than on most courses I have taken.
36. I had a strong desire to take this course.
37. I would like to take another course from this instructor.
38. As a result of taking this course, I have more positive feelings toward this field of study.
39. I have given thoughtful consideration to the questions on this form.

● Describe your status on the following by blackening the appropriate space on the Response Card.

A. To which sex-age group do you belong?
1 — Female, under 25   3 — Female, 25 or over
2 — Male, under 25   4 — Male, 25 or over

B. Do you consider yourself to be a full-time or a part-time student?
1 — Full-time
2 — Part-time

C. Counting the present term, for how many terms have you attended this college or university?
1 — 1 term   3 — 4 or 5
2 — 2 or 3   4 — 6 or more

D. What grade do you expect to receive in this course?
1 — A   3 — C
2 — B   4 — D or F   5 — Other

E. What is your classification?
1 — Freshman   3 — Junior or Senior
2 — Sophomore   4 — Graduate   5 — Other

F. For how many courses have you filled out this form during the present term?
1 — This is the first course
2 — 2 or 3 courses   3 — 4 or more courses

G. How well did the questions on this form permit you to describe your impressions of this instructor and course?
1 — Very well   3 — Not very well
2 — Quite well   4 — Poorly

If your instructor has extra questions, answer them in the space designated on the Response Card.

Your comments are invited on how the instructor might improve this course or teaching procedures. Use the back of the Response Card (unless otherwise directed).

Exhibit 7. Factors or Categories of Ratings and Examples of Items

1. Organization, Structure, or Clarity
   - Material presented in an orderly manner
   - Instructor well prepared for each class
   - Class time well spent
   - Course well organized
   - Instructor made clear what we were expected to learn
   - Considerable agreement between announced objectives and what was taught

2. Teacher-Student Interaction or Rapport
   - Instructor readily available for consultation with students
   - Instructor seemed to know when students didn't understand the material
   - Instructor actively helpful when students had difficulty
   - Students felt free to ask questions or express opinions
   - Instructor seemed concerned with whether students learned the material

3. Teaching Skill, Communication, or Lecturing Ability
   - Instructor used examples or illustrations to clarify the material
   - Instructor spoke audibly and clearly
   - Instructor presented material clearly
   - Instructor summarized or emphasized major points in lectures or discussions

4. Workload, Course Difficulty
   - In relation to other courses, this workload was heavy
   - Instructor tried to cover too much material
   - Reading assignments were very difficult
   - Course challenged me intellectually
   - I put a great deal of effort into this course

5. Grading, Examinations
   - Instructor told students how they would be evaluated
   - Examinations reflected the important aspects of the course
   - Instructor made helpful comments on papers or exams
   - Instructor assigned grades fairly and impartially

6. Impact on Students, Student Self-Rated Accomplishments
   - I learned a great deal in this course
   - This course generally fulfilled my goals
   - This course stimulated me to want to take more work in the same or a related area

7. Global, Overall Ratings
   - Instructor's effectiveness as a teacher was: (excellent to poor)
   - Overall value of the course was: (excellent to poor)
   - Instructor made a major contribution to the value of this course
   - General quality of lectures was: (excellent to poor)
   - General quality of class discussions was: (excellent to poor)

sponsible for such problems. An alternate approach is to ask students to rate individually their progress toward each specific content objective.

In format, most rating instruments encourage students to add comments about the course and the way it was taught. Open-ended questions—such as "How do you think the course can be improved?" or "What did you like least (and most) about the course?"—can be used to elicit student reactions that single-response questions fail to tap. Some instructors and departments prefer to use such open-ended questions. Students might understandably feel constrained, however, about making negative comments, fearing that their course grades would be affected; typing would ensure anonymity, but the cost and time involved in this practice limits its use. Responses to open-ended questions are also vulnerable to more subjective interpretation than are answers to single-response questions. If the comments are used in a summary evaluation of the instructor, care must be taken not to put undue weight on a few highly negative or highly positive remarks.

Including an optional section or open-ended questions on rating forms allows instructors greater flexibility in improving the course and their teaching practices. Another way to give individual teachers some flexibility and choice, devised at Purdue University, is known as the "cafeteria system" (see the Appendix). This computer-assisted system allows teachers to choose from a catalogue listing 200 items. Selections are added to a nonoptional core of five items, and the computer prints individually designed questionnaires. As with standard forms, the computer then scores and processes student responses. Other institutions such as the University of Illinois and the University of Michigan have similar rating programs.

Although the major use of student ratings is to guide instructional improvement and faculty summative evaluations, another use is to help students in their choice of courses and teachers. Forms for this use include items rating the evaluation of class sessions, the relevance of the course, the amount of work required, and the degree of teacher interest in the class. Such information is also useful to teachers for course improvement. In practice, most of the items typically found in forms designed for student use are included in instruments designed for teacher use, so the contents of the two types of instruments generally differ much less than do their intended audiences.

Some student government groups and other student organizations collect and publish student rating information. As might be expected, student-produced critiques vary considerably in quality from one institution to another and from one year to the next, depending on the students involved. A few student-sponsored rating programs allow teachers to see their personal ratings prior to publication in order to include their comments on the findings or to provide additional information about the courses. This approach is more impartial, and it provides information about the courses that is not usually found in college catalogues. Unfortunately, certain student-sponsored course critiques are based on ratings by small and nonrepresentative samples of students or may emphasize some of the more critical comments about a teacher, regardless of how generalized such comments may be, thus leading many faculty members to object to student-conducted course ratings. Critics also argue that student-sponsored ratings result in "instructor hostility, resentment, and distrust," and thus alienate faculty members from their work with the class (Kerlinger, 1971, p. 354).

A recent and less common use of student ratings is to determine whether or not teachers possess the minimal competencies and behaviors expected of all faculty members. At Michigan State University, for example, the Academic Council approved a code of teaching responsibility that included seven specific provisions recommended for use in making salary, promotion, and tenure decisions. The council also approved a student rating form to reflect specific points in the code, including the following (Olson, 1977):

1. Were the instructional objectives stated either in writing or orally at the beginning of the term? Was instruction consistent with stated objectives?
2. Did the instructor explain course grading procedures either in writing or orally? Were the stated grading procedures followed?
3. Were graded materials returned to you soon enough to be useful in your learning?
4. Did the instructor meet your class at the scheduled or agreed upon time?
5. Did the instructor have scheduled office hours for consultation? Was the instructor or teaching assistant available during office hours?

6. Was the instructor available for prearranged appointments with you?

The vast majority of faculty members would receive positive responses to these and other items on the form. For the few who might not, the information obtained would be useful in making administrative decisions and in enforcing a reasonable teaching code.

Regardless of their purpose, student rating forms should be succinct. Ten to fifteen minutes should be the maximum time needed to complete a set of questions; anything longer strains student interest and tolerance and diminishes the quality of responses, especially if forms have been completed for several courses. As teachers, too, would resent too much class time being spent in this way, institutions might offer them a short form of no more than ten questions. A slightly longer form designed particularly for instructional improvement could be administered when teachers want more detailed information.

Are Student Ratings Reliable?

An instrument of poor reliability can be thought of as an elastic yardstick that would provide a different reading each time it was used. Student ratings are not elastic yardsticks. Their reliability or consistency, as indicated by numerous studies, is very good, providing enough students in a class have made ratings. For personnel decisions, it is also important to base judgments on several courses taught by a specific teacher.

Feldman (1977) discussed several procedures used by researchers to determine the reliability of student ratings. Each procedure estimates the extent of student agreement on ratings within a class or their internal consistency. The results are fairly similar, regardless of the specific procedure. One method draws pairs of students at random from a course and correlates their ratings, with higher correlations indicating greater consistency among student respondents. A similar method computes the mean scores for random halves of a class and then correlates these means across a number of classes. A third and more frequently used method computes the intraclass correlation coefficient (Winer, 1962). This index compares the variation within classes with the variation across classes to provide an estimate of the relative homogeneity of ratings. A low reliability estimate, according to this method, usually indicates a wide variation in ratings among students in a typical class. Ideally, it is desirable to have more differentiation among mean scores for teachers than among individual student responses in each class. As with the other procedures, this does not measure the extent to which students give exactly the same rating.

Applying the intraclass correlation procedure, I calculated reliabilities for each of thirty instructional rating items and for varying numbers of student raters (Centra, 1973a). With ten raters, the reliability coefficients were about .70 for most items and .78 for ratings of a teacher's overall effectiveness. The estimated reliability for fifteen student raters was above .80 for most of the items; for twenty raters, the reliabilities were close to .90. These average reliabilities are similar to those reported in other studies.

Given this information, how many students are needed to provide a sound basis for a reliable average rating? The answer depends on how the rating results are to be used. For instructional improvements, average ratings based on as few as eight or ten students could provide the instructor with useful information, but larger numbers are preferable. To evaluate a teacher's instructional effectiveness for a promotional decision, both the number of students rating each course and the number of courses to be considered are critical. A study by Gilmore, Kane, and Naccarato (1978) shows that the use of ratings from five or more courses in which some fifteen students responded will result in a "dependable" assessment of teaching effectiveness; they found that ratings from more than five courses are required for dependability if teachers have taught relatively small sections (fewer than fifteen students). If as many as ten courses are considered, then the number of student raters for the various courses makes little difference. If the ratings of only one or two courses are considered, however, the researchers concluded that the results should not be used as a measure of teaching effectiveness for personnel decisions, regardless of the number of raters.

The proportion of a class that rates an instructor is as important as the number of raters. If only twenty out of sixty students in a class respond to a rating form, it is possible that they do not represent the reactions of the entire class (unless raters are selected on a random basis). Even with responses from two thirds of the enrolled students in a course—the minimum desirable proportion—there could be some response bias. Using the evaluations of a sufficient number of students, however, will reduce the effects of a few divergent raters.

The stability of student responses has also been investigated to determine the influence of student moods and other invalid effects. Rating forms given twice to the same students over a short period of time produced fairly stable results (Costin, 1968; Centra, 1972); the mean ratings for 296 teachers collected about five weeks apart, for example, correlated an average of .70 for twenty-three rating items. Ratings collected a year apart from the same students also correlated significantly, though the later ratings tended to rate the teacher as less effective than those collected at the end of the course (Overall and Marsh, 1978).

Do Student and Class Characteristics Affect Student Ratings?

The fact that student ratings are reasonably reliable and stable when based on responses from a sufficiently large sample of students does not guarantee that they are immune from contamination. Whether the ratings actually assess teaching behavior or reflect characteristics of (1) a course over which the teacher has little control or (2) of the raters themselves are critical questions—especially when ratings are used administratively. Student characteristics that could affect ratings include: age, sex, college year (freshman, sophomore, and so on), academic ability, grade point average, expected grade in the course, reason for taking the course, and personality differences. Course characteristics that could have an effect include: type of course requirement (major requirement, general college requirement, or elective), subject matter area, class size, and method of instruction. The relationship between these factors and student ratings has been investigated in hundreds of studies, several of which are reviewed by Costin, Greenough, and Menges (1971), Kulik and McKeachie (1975), and Doyle (1975).

For a closer look at the possible effects of student and course factors on ratings, we drew on responses from over 300,000 students and approximately 16,000 classes at over 100 colleges that had used the Student Instructional Report (Centra and Creech, 1976). To facilitate computations, a random sample of approximately 15,000 students and 9,000 classes was selected and analyzed, focusing on the following five-point global question: Compared to other instructors you have had (secondary school and college), how effective has the instructor been in this course?

- One of the most effective (among the top 10 percent)
- More effective than most (among the top 30 percent)
- About average
- Not as effective as most (in the lowest 30 percent)
- One of the least effective (in the lowest 10 percent)

Findings from this survey were similar to those from many other studies: the relationships between student or course characteristics and student ratings were generally insignificant or small enough not to have any practical significance. For several factors, however—class size, subject area of the course, and (occasionally) the course in relation to the students' curriculum—the correlations with ratings were high enough to recommend that they be considered in interpreting ratings.

Student characteristics having weak or insignificant relationships with ratings of teacher effectiveness were: sex, grade point average, college year, academic ability, and age. For example, the mean ratings given by females and males were almost identical: 3.74 and 3.73. But this is not to say that teachers who direct their teaching toward students of a particular sex or ability level will not be rated differently by those groups, as Elliot (1950) suggests. He finds a positive correlation between grade point averages and teacher ratings only when the teacher taught to the better students in the class. Another study (Centra and Linn, 1976) analyzed separately the student ratings within each of three large classes. Subgroups of students in each of the three classes rated differently such things as course examinations, class discussions, and assignments, but in only one of the courses (titled [significantly?] "Social Inequality") did such student characteristics as grades, gender, and college year differentiate the subgroups. Similarly, Yonge and Sassenrath (1968) investigated the relationship between student personality factors and ratings for each of three instructors; they found personality factors to be somewhat related to ratings, but the relationships were not consistent for all three instructors.

These analyses within classes, as well as the numerous studies based on data pooled across classes, indicate that student characteristics, although not systematically affecting the ratings given, may on occasion have a significant effect. Teachers who use ratings for self-improvement thus may find it useful to look beyond the average ratings from the entire class and inspect the responses of identifiable subgroups of students, such as those with high or low grade point averages. By examining subgroups' responses, instructors may discover a rating pattern that suggests that one segment of the class is being slighted. If so, some adjustments in teaching methods or course design may be needed.

In personnel decisions, ratings should span a number of courses taught by a particular instructor in order to reduce the likelihood that the ratings have been systematically biased for or against the instructor. Providing norms or comparison information for similar courses can be equally valuable. This is especially important for factors, including the following four, that are more highly related to ratings.

Class Size. Very small classes—those with less than ten or fifteen students—are most highly rated. Those with fewer than fifteen students clearly received the highest ratings, followed by those with sixteen to thirty-five students and those with over a hundred students. The lowest ratings are found in classes with thirty-five to a hundred students (Centra and Creech, 1976). Classes of more than a hundred students may receive higher ratings because colleges or departments assign their best teachers and resources to such large classes and because the teachers themselves may prepare more thoroughly for particularly large groups of students than they would for smaller ones. Classes with thirty-five to a hundred students may not receive such attention and may also be too large to facilitate teacher-student interaction. Smaller classes, especially those with fewer than fifteen students and thus with fewer demands and less student variation, allow more questions to be posed and answered and enable teachers to adjust material more closely to student needs than do larger classes. For the same reasons, discussion courses are generally rated higher in both course value and teacher effectiveness than are lecture courses.

Subject Matter. In comparing thousands of classes in each of the fields of study, slightly higher student ratings of course value and teacher effectiveness are found in the fields of the humanities than in the social sciences and the natural sciences (Centra and Creech, 1976; Educational Testing Service, 1975, 1977). Why this general pattern exists is not clear, but it may be due to the relative importance accorded to teaching and to research by instructors in each of the different fields. In one study (Parsons and Platt, 1968), teachers in the natural sciences judged research to be three times as important as teaching and social science teachers saw research as being "four thirds" as important as teaching; only in the humanities did instructors see research and teaching as equal in importance.

Students in more than four hundred classes from five colleges rated courses in the natural sciences as faster paced, more difficult, and less stimulating than those in the humanities, social sciences, and education (Centra, 1972). They reported natural science teachers to be less open to new viewpoints than teachers in other disciplines. Humanities teachers, compared to those in the other three areas, were rated as less likely to inform students of evaluation methods and less likely to teach toward announced objectives.

Type of Course Requirement. Students give slightly higher ratings to their majors or electives than to courses taken to fulfill a college requirement (Centra and Creech, 1976). Their motivation and their personal interest in their major courses and in subjects they have chosen to study would lead them to rate the courses as more valuable and effective. In addition, some teachers have less interest in lower-level, college-required courses and thus put less effort into their teaching.

Grade Expected. Of major concern in rating programs are the influence of students' grades on their ratings and the possibility that students will reward easy-grading teachers with higher ratings. There seems to be no overriding evidence that students rate an instructor more favorably or unfavorably on the basis of the grades they anticipate receiving—although there may be occasions when that occurs, as shown by Holmes (1972), who found that students give the instructor lower ratings if their actual grades are lower than those they had expected. Similarly, they give lower ratings when their expected grade is lower than the grades they have received in other courses, as indicated by their cumulative grade point average (Bausell and Magoon, 1972; Centra and Creech, 1976).

The correlation between grades and ratings is usually in the .20 range. In one study (Centra and Creech, 1976), students expecting an A grade gave teachers an average rating of 3.95 (on a five-point scale), while those expecting a C grade gave them an average rating of 3.41. The correlation between expected grade and student ratings of the course value are generally a little higher than the correlation between expected grade and teacher rating. Both correlations are based on data pooled across classes, but evidence indicates that the same relationships would hold for analyses within classes as well (Centra and Linn, 1976).

One way to interpret the association between expected grade and ratings is to view it as partial evidence for validity: If a grade or an expected grade reflects how much a student knows about the subject matter at the end of the course, then there should be some relationship between that grade and the student's ratings of the teacher and of the course. In part, then, the relationship can be viewed as modest evidence that students rate higher those courses in which they learn more.

Are Ratings Affected by Teacher Characteristics?

Whether student ratings reflect characteristics of instructors that should have no effect on their teaching effectiveness is a major concern. (We would hope, for example, that students would not rate full professors highly simply because of their rank or status on campus.) Research evidence indicates that teacher characteristics are generally not related to the ratings they receive. The one exception is the number of years of teaching experience, but the pattern of ratings for teachers with varying years of experience is clearly explainable and probably does not reflect bias.

Analysis of the ratings of overall teaching effectiveness for more than 8,000 teachers with varying years of experience shows that those in their first year of teaching generally receive the poorest ratings (average 3.54 on a five-point scale [Centra and Creech, 1976]). Teachers with one or two years of experience and those with more than twelve years receive similar ratings, an average of about 3.75. Slightly higher are teachers in the three- to twelve-year range, with an average of 3.83. First-year teachers are usually learning on the job; most of them have had little formal training in graduate school on the process of teaching. In using ratings for administrative purposes, then, it should be recognized that first-year teachers may improve considerably with experience. While instructors with very poor ratings may not become exceptional teachers, there could be critical changes for first-year teachers who receive only average ratings.

The slight decline in rated effectiveness in the later years of a teaching career (there is no significance in the twelfth year per se; my recent analysis with a new sample indicates that teachers with over twenty years of experience received even lower ratings on the average) has implications for teaching improvement programs. Some teachers acquire substantial administrative or research responsibilities in their later years, along with a decline in teaching involvement; others become bored and indifferent. Faculty development programs, therefore, need to be concerned with revitalizing older teachers and with assisting those just entering the profession. Highet (1976) points out that changes occur over time in the subject matter within a discipline, as do teachers' relationships with their students. He believes that many teachers in their later years assume too much knowledge on the part of the young, while their own grasp of the subject matter has become more automatic. Eble (1971) provides an excellent discussion of career development for faculty members in mid-career and later.

Numerous studies have correlated other teacher characteristics with ratings, such as academic rank, sex, teaching load, and research productivity. None of these, however, are significantly and consistently related to ratings.

Academic Rank. The mean scores for more than 8,000 teachers at four academic ranks (instructor through professor) are virtually identical (Centra and Creech, 1976). Only teaching assistants received significantly lower scores—probably due to their limited teaching experience, as discussed earlier.

Sex. Male and female teachers are occasionally rated differently, but the differences do not have much practical significance. Students in one study (Centra, 1972) rated women teachers higher than men teachers on items dealing with teacher–student interaction; however, they found courses taught by men more stimulating. A few studies reported ratings to be slightly higher when teacher and student gender are the same (Ferber and Huber, 1975; Elmore and LaPointe, 1975), but even these small differences are inconsistent and may depend on the particular course (Wilson and Doyle, 1976).

Teaching Load. One might expect that faculty members with the heaviest teaching loads would receive lower student ratings because of less time for preparation and other teaching-related activities. Yet the opposite is true. Analysis of ratings for the more than 8,000 teachers studied by Centra and Creech (1976) indicates that teachers with a credit-hour load of thirteen or more were given the highest ratings. There is little difference in the ratings of teachers with less than a thirteen-hour teaching load. Faculty with loads of thirteen or more hours are generally located at two-year or four-year colleges where teaching is the major faculty activity. Indeed, the ratings of teachers at two-year colleges are slightly higher than for teachers at four-year colleges and universities (Educational Testing Service, 1975, 1977). For teachers at the same college or at the same type of college, teaching load would probably have little effect on ratings and need not be considered in their interpretation. Some colleges, however, do take teaching load into account in determining faculty rewards and promotions (see Chapter Eight).

Research Productivity. Research and writing help to keep teachers refreshed and on top of their fields, a good reason to expect a positive relationship between scholarly productivity and teaching effectiveness as assessed by students. A few studies support this expectation (see Stallings and Singhal, 1970). Several other studies, however, report no association between research productivity—as reflected by the numbers of books and articles published—and student ratings of teaching effectiveness (see Guthrie, 1954; Voeks, 1962; Aleamoni and Yimer, 1973). Publications apparently are not essential for good teaching; therefore the use of publication counts in teacher evaluation will not reflect teaching performance as judged by students. Publications also appear to be unrelated to colleague ratings of teaching (Aleamoni and Yimer, 1973).

Are Teachers Who "Entertain" Rather than "Teach"
Rated Highly by Students?

This question, frequently raised by faculty members, raises an important issue: what students perceive as good teaching. A study by Naftulin, Ware, and Donnelly (1973) tested the entertainment question by employing a professional actor to deliver a graduate-level lecture that was nonsubstantive and contradictory in content. Dr. Fox, as the actor was called, was a very entertaining and dynamic lecturer. The high ratings that he received, the researchers reasoned, supported their contention that "Given a sufficiently impressive lecture paradigm, an experienced group of educators participating in a new learning situation can feel satisfied that they have learned despite irrelevant, conflicting, and meaningless content conveyed by the lecturer" (1973, p. 634).

The students gave Dr. Fox high ratings in organization, stimulation, and interest in the subject—probably accurate reflections of the actor's performance. It was the content of the lecture that was faulty. In a sense, then, the Dr. Fox results underscore findings from other studies showing "lecturing ability" to be an important part of teaching effectiveness as rated by students. Many of them rate a good teacher as one who has a great deal of interest and enthusiasm in the subject, organizes the material well, and is stimulating in presentation. So is a good entertainer. To some extent, then, teaching and entertainment do overlap, at least in lecture presentations. But, as Guthrie (1954) found, highly rated teachers tend to be "substance teachers" and not merely good entertainers. The Costin, Greenough, and Menges (1971) conclusion would still seem applicable: sheer "entertainment" is not what most students see as good teaching.

The Dr. Fox study has implications as to who should evaluate a teacher's knowledge of subject matter. Given the fact that the study was based on only one lecture, it is conceivable that the students would eventually have rated the content as poor. Certainly it is much easier to delude a group of students for one session than for an entire semester. Even so, the results support the view that colleagues are more appropriate than students as judges of a teacher's subject knowledge.

Do Students Learn More from Teachers Whom They Rate Highly?

Global ratings of teacher effectiveness and course value correlate more highly with student learning than do the ratings of such
specific instructional practices as teacher–student interaction. Global
ratings may be more valid estimates of student learning because they
are not tied to a specific instructional style. The research results also
suggest that some instructional practices work well for some teachers
but not all. Close student relationships are not needed by all teachers,
for example, to facilitate learning in their courses. For some it is part
of their teaching style, and it may well contribute to their effectiveness
as measured by ratings or student achievement. Other practices may
account for the effectiveness of other teachers. This means that in
using ratings in personnel decisions, global ratings could be more
defensible than ratings of specific practices. Although global ratings
and achievement are generally correlated highly for most courses in
the studies, the exceptions underscore the need to supplement ratings
with additional criteria of teaching effectiveness.

Are highly rated teachers those from whom students learn
most? This question focuses on the critical issue of what student
ratings actually mean. It has spawned numerous validity studies that
employ the so-called criterion-related approach to validity: the
amount that students have learned at the end of a course is the
criterion of good teaching—an argument with strong support (for
example, Cohen and Brawer, 1969; Rose, 1976). Student ratings,
hopefully, will be at least moderately related to learning. Multisection
courses with common final examinations in each are used for these
studies; for each section, mean student ratings are correlated with
mean final exam performance at the end of the course. Students
generally select their sections or teachers rather than being assigned at
random, which requires some kind of statistical adjustment to com-
pensate for initial differences in student ability or achievement. For
example, Elliot (1950) adjusted for academic aptitude and found
moderate correlations between the adjusted achievement scores and
ratings of some aspects of instruction. Cohen and Berger (1970),
Morsh, Burgess, and Smith (1956), McKeachie, Lin, and Mann (1971),
and Doyle and Whitely (1974) also report moderate correlations be-

tween ratings and learning, but again students were not assigned to teachers on a random basis.

A high negative correlation between learning and ratings is reported by Rodin and Rodin (1972), who found that students actually learned *less* from teachers whom they rated highly. Because of this unusual result—and probably because of its publication in *Science*— the study received a great deal of undeserved attention. The sample studied consisted of twelve teaching assistants who were teaching in only a peripheral sense: they met with their classes two days a week (the professor lectured to the entire group on the other three), primarily to help those students who needed aid in solving assigned calculus problems. Since the Rodins used as their criterion the number of calculus problems done correctly by students at the end of the term, the negative relationship with ratings is understandable. It is likely that students who had little need of help not only obtained the best grades but also rated the teaching assistant lowest in teaching performance (they may, in fact, have skipped many class sessions). Students most in need of help solved the fewest number of problems and probably rated their teachers highest. In other words, aid provided by the teaching assistant—or teaching performance—may have had little to do with the number of problems that students completed.

A proper study includes teachers in more typical multisection instructional settings and also includes a random assignment of students to each class section. Randomization helps to ensure that differences in final exam scores will be due to teacher effectiveness rather than to differences in student motivation. Highly motivated students might do better than was predicted by a pretest and might seek out teachers with good reputations and rate them higher regardless of teaching performance (Leventhal, 1975). In short, randomization of students is one of the steps needed to draw a cause and effect relationship between rated teacher effectiveness and student learning.

In two studies (Sullivan and Skanes, 1974; Centra, 1977b), students were assigned at random to multisection courses in which a common final examination was used. The Centra study also included some courses in which randomization was not used. Both studies took place at Memorial University in Newfoundland and together included analyses of 202 sections in seventeen courses—the subject areas being first-year chemistry, biology, mathematics, physics, and psychology. Sullivan and Skanes report that the average correlation between ratings of teacher competence and student learning as measured by the final exam was modest but significant: .39. The relationship, however, was much higher for full-time instructors (.53) than for teaching assistants (.01), and for experienced teachers (.69) versus those in their first year of teaching (.13). Inexperienced teachers, Sullivan and Skanes reason, have not yet developed a consistent teaching style, thereby contributing to the low validity correlation.

The Centra analysis finds a significant relationship between ratings of teacher effectiveness and student achievement: half of the correlations are .60 or higher and all but one are positive. Student ratings of the course value show similar results. Ratings of course objectives, of organization, and of the quality of lectures correlate fairly well with achievement. Ratings of the teacher–student relationship, of course examinations, and of student effort do not correlate strongly with achievement: the median correlation is .30. The weakest or most inconsistent correlations with achievement are for ratings of teaching assignments and for course difficulty and workload.

The relationships between ratings and student achievement are significant, but they might have been higher if the range for both types of variables was greater. The restricted range of achievement scores between the sections and the limited variability in mean ratings across instructors, evident in both studies, suppress the correlations.

Do Student Ratings Improve Instruction?

There is a good deal of skepticism regarding the effect of student ratings on changes or improvements in instruction—particularly when the results are seen only by the individual teacher. It is assumed that teachers value student opinion enough to alter their instructional practices when needed. But do they? Although the ratings that individual teachers receive often improve over time, it cannot be assumed that the initial ratings caused that improvement; additional teaching experience by itself often results in instructional changes. Student ratings may lead to some changes when only the teachers see the results, but there are probably many ways to increase their impact.

To investigate the effects of student ratings on a teacher's practices requires an experimental design in which random groups of teachers receive feedback from students while other teachers—those in control groups—do not. Such a study (Centra, 1973b) involved more than 400 teachers at five different types of college. In every department, teachers were randomly assigned to one of three groups: (1) *The feedback group*, in which teachers administered the student rating form at midsemester and received a summary of the results within a week, along with some comparison data to aid in interpretation. In research terms this is the "treatment" group, the treatment in this instance being what is done at most colleges using student ratings for instructional improvement—the results are seen only by the instructor. (2) *The no-feedback group* used the rating form at midsemester but saw the summary of results at the end of the semester. This is the "control" group. (3) *The post-test group*, in which the rating form was used only at the end of the semester to determine whether midsemester ratings had a sensitizing effect on teachers in the no-feedback group—whether their use of the form resulted in changes even though they had not had any feedback.

In addition to using the form at midsemester, teachers in the feedback and no-feedback groups administered the form at the end of the semester. Both sets of ratings were collected during the single 1971 fall semester, so that the same students could provide both sets of ratings. Teachers were also asked at midsemester to rate their own instructional practices on a self-rating form that paralleled the student rating form.

The major conclusion of the study is that, for instructors whose self-evaluations were considerably better than were their student ratings, changes in instruction (as assessed by repeated student evaluations) occur after only a half semester. If, in other words, teachers are "unrealistic" in observing their teaching—unrealistic relative to their students' view, that is—then they tend to make changes in their instructional practices. A second finding is that a wider variety of instructors change if given more than a half semester of time and if they have information to help them interpret their scores. These changes are most evident in their preparation for class, use of class time, summarization of major points in lectures or discussions,

openness to other viewponts, and making helpful comments on
papers or exams.

The reason to relate changes in teaching procedures to the
discrepancy between self-evaluation and student ratings can be found
in social-psychological theory—in particular, in equilibrium or self-
consistency theory, the central notion of which is that an individual's
actions are strongly influenced by self-evaluation. Thus, when student
ratings are much poorer than an instructor's self-rating, a condition
of imbalance (Heider, 1958) or dissonance (Festinger, 1957) is created
in the instructor. In an attempt to become more consistent—or, in
theoretical terms, to restore a condition of equilibrium—the instructor
changes in the direction suggested by the student ratings.

These theories assume that most teachers value collective student ratings and that they know how to make changes. The study
results indicate that to some extent this occurs. Undoubtedly, however,
some teachers write off student judgment as unreliable or unworthy,
and for these individuals changes are unlikely even though they may
be needed. Other types of evaluation or analysis may be more effective
for these teachers, such as colleague reactions or use of in-class
videotapes.

Still other means of treating student rating responses might
have greater impact. If instructors rate themselves on most items, it is
possible to produce a discrepancy score between student and self-
ratings that can highlight aspects of instruction in special need of
attention. Publicizing ratings may also draw increased attention to
them. Response summaries in the five colleges studied (Centra, 1973b)
were seen only by the individual teacher; publicized ratings might
have pressured more teachers to change their methods. Including
ratings in personnel decisions will also increase their importance,
though some instructors may not know how to go about improving
their teaching methods. It is therefore possible to use ratings in a
counseling situation as part of a faculty or instructional development
program. According to some research evidence (Aleamoni, 1974),
accompanying rating results with some kind of counsel—such as that
of a faculty development specialist or a master teacher—is effective.

The impact of ratings can be increased by evaluating continuously rather than only at the end of the course. Parent and others
(1971) describe a program tried at the University of Minnesota. The

instructor plans the course content and instructional methods on what he or she has learned of student expectations at the start of the course, their prior preparation, and personal descriptive information. A course and instructional rating form at midterm elicits student reactions to course content and organization, the adequacy of methods used, the value of texts and assignments, and the like. In addition, six to ten students act as ombudsmen, funneling the reactions of other students to the teacher. According to the authors, this procedure has the advantages of involving students directly in course development, of providing teachers with information that allows them to adapt course content to the enrolled students, and of promoting good relationships between students and faculty—thus increasing student motivation and learning experiences.

Do Alumni Rate Teachers Differently?

It is frequently said that student ratings do not adequately reflect the long-term effects of instruction. Student immaturity or lack of perspective are often blamed for this shortcoming, and it is assumed that later ratings—say, when the students are alumni—are more valid measures of teacher effectiveness. There is the example of the hard-driving, demanding teacher supposedly not appreciated by students until they have gained more real-life experience. Though there may be times when this is indeed the case, research suggests that it is rare; most teachers rated poorly by students are also rated poorly by alumni.

Because of the general agreement between student and alumni ratings, there seems to be little need to use the latter in faculty tenure and promotion decisions. Ratings by current students provide similar information and are much easier to collect. Alumni ratings are also less useful in instructional improvement since alumni may not be able to recall the kind of specific information needed by teachers. Alumni, on the other hand, may be able to provide useful reactions to the relevance of courses in the curriculum and to other college experiences, reactions which could be useful in modifying department offerings.

Three studies demonstrate the similarity between student and alumni ratings of instruction. Drucker and Remmers (1951) surveyed graduates who had been out of college for ten or more years and found positive correlations between ratings given to seventeen instructors by students and alumni. Correlations ranged from .40 to .68 on ten such teacher traits as the presentation of student matter, interest in the subject, sympathetic attitude toward students, and fairness in grading. Had these correlations been based on an overall assessment of teaching rather than of specific traits and had the length of time away from the courses not been as great, they might have been higher. Student ratings of overall teacher effectiveness compared with similar ratings by alumni who had been out no more than five years (Centra, 1974) showed agreement between the two. In this study, some 500 alumni named the best and worst teachers they had had in college. The rank correlation for student and alumni responses based on the ratings for twenty-three teachers was .75. The agreement between current studies and alumni regarding specific effective or ineffective teachers thus was substantial, particularly at the extremes: very good and very poor teachers were identified as such by both students and alumni.

In some instances, however, a teacher was seen as both "good" and "bad" by the same groups; the same teacher was occasionally nominated as one of the best teachers by some alumni and as one of the worst by other alumni. Obviously, some teachers have a special appeal or lack of appeal to specific kinds of students. Other researchers indicate that it is not enough to speak just of "good" or "bad" teachers; one might also ask "good" or "bad" for which students (McKeachie, Lin, and Mann, 1971; Dowaliby and Schumer, 1973). While this admonition would seem justified for some of the teachers in the Centra (1974) study of alumni ratings, most teachers in the sample appeared to be effective with a wide variety of students—at least, as measured by a single overall rating provided by alumni and students.

A third study of long-term effects of instruction (Overall and Marsh, 1978) compares responses from alumni who had rated a senior-level course with their ratings of the course and instructor a year after graduation. Although the alumni ratings tend to be lower than ratings given at the end of the course, the two sets of ratings are consistent in that they correlate significantly. Unlike the previous two studies, the same individuals rated the teacher at both times.

Are Student Ratings Affected by Their Intended Use?

Because of the serious implications for the teacher, one might expect students to rate the teacher more leniently if the results are to be considered in salary, tenure, or promotion deliberations. On the other hand, they might be more frank and perhaps more severe in their ratings and criticism if the results are to be used for course or instructional improvement; such information, they might logically assume, could lead to needed changes.

Ratings collected in forty-one classes at a midwestern university showed that students tend to rate teachers similarly under both circumstances (Centra, 1976b). Random halves of each of the classes were given different written directions regarding the intended use of the results—i.e., "will be used in *salary, promotion or tenure* considerations for this teacher," or "will be used *only by the instructor* to evaluate and improve his or her teaching." A comparison of responses indicated that only in a few instances did students give more favorable ratings when they understood that the results would be used administratively. Later studies reported similar results, so the findings seem to be valid.

Although the small differences in ratings indicate that students are generally not influenced by written instructions, it may well be that oral directions given by a teacher, especially if given with a subtle appeal to generosity, could have a sizable effect. A study by Fentress and Swanson (1973) found that instructors got higher ratings by giving reinforcement and praise to the class at the time the forms were administered. They also found that the teaching assistants who participated in the study could influence their ratings favorably by combining praise of the class with outright reinforcement in the form of soft drinks, pretzels, and potato chips.

Should Ratings Be Anonymous?

To use ratings for tenure, promotion, or salary considerations, it is advisable to establish standardized procedures for the administration of forms, procedures such as the requirement that a student or some type of proctor distribute, collect, and place the questionnaires in a sealed envelope and that the teachers not be present during the administration of the questionnaires. It is advisable also to keep rating forms anonymous in all cases, thus ensuring that a student cannot be penalized for giving low ratings.

Some teachers argue that signed rating forms motivate students to give thoughtful responses and allow teachers to obtain detailed information from selected students regarding critical responses. And, if ratings are used for administrative purposes, they argue that they should know their accusers—a specious argument, since only the average class ratings are reliable and not individual student responses. Although students who identify themselves are expected to be far more generous in their ratings, especially if the forms are distributed and returned to the instructor prior to final grading, evidence does not totally support this expectation. One study finds that students who identify themselves rate their teachers no differently than those who remain anonymous (Stone, Rabinowitz, and Spool, 1977), while another study by the same researchers finds the expected higher ratings by students who completed signed rating forms (Stone, Spool, and Rabinowitz, 1977).

What Are the Limitations on Student Ratings?

Limitations of student rating programs other than those already given in this chapter should be considered:

1. Because most student rating instruments elicit numerical responses that can be scored and quantified, it is easy to assign them a precision they do not possess. In a discussion of standardized tests, Turnbull (1978) terms this tendency the "micrometer fallacy." Decision makers therefore should guard against overinterpreting small variations between teachers; there is little practical difference between a teacher whose mean rating is at the 60th percentile and another who is at the 65th percentile. Another fault is giving student ratings too much weight in relation to other criteria. Because they can be quantified, the temptation to assign them undue importance is understandable.

2. The manipulations of ratings by teachers must be considered when ratings are used for personnel decisions. At issue is whether

teachers can influence ratings but not student learning. Teachers who argue, as one did, that they can improve their ratings by inviting students to their homes for informal discussion accompanied by refreshments can also be improving student learning and motivation as well. Their attempt to improve ratings is, in this instance, also a good educational practice. But the teacher who is lenient in assigning grades and out-of-class work is not improving learning, yet may be better rated by some students. The extent to which lenient grading consistently causes higher ratings is still in question. As one safeguard, a teacher's grade distribution ought to be examined; in particular, the course grades for students in the class should be compared with their average grades in other courses. An inflation-proof grading system along these lines has been proposed at the University of California, Berkeley (Carnegie Council on Policy Studies in Higher Education, 1979).

3. Some institutions point to their student rating system as proof that they are concerned about improving teaching yet do little else to help teachers develop their skills. In short, student ratings have misled some institutions into thinking that nothing more is needed to upgrade instruction. While some teachers can use the rating information to make needed changes, others need faculty and instructional development services.

4. Because of the positive bias in student ratings, teachers who need to improve may not realize their weaknesses. Providing comparative data is one way to minimize misleading interpretations.

Recommendations

1. For personnel decisions, ratings of a teacher across courses should be considered, the minimum number of courses depending on the number of student raters in each course. In general, five or more courses are needed for a dependable assessment if at least fifteen students have rated each course.

2. Do not overuse student ratings. Students will get bored and will respond haphazardly or not at all. Use can be limited by recommending that tenured staff collect ratings in only one course each year and in new courses; nontenured staff could collect ratings in their different courses but not in every section.

3. A rating form should not be excessively long. Ten minutes to complete a form is all most students will want to spend, and teachers are often reluctant to use up too much class time.

4. For personnel decisions, items that rate the overall effectiveness of the teacher and course (global items) are especially useful. Other items might be used in making judgments if they reflect a teaching code that all teachers are expected to fulfill.

5. If a common set of rating items are adopted or developed by a college, teachers and departments should have the option of adding their own specific items. Written comments by students should also be encouraged for instructional and course improvement.

6. Decision makers and teachers need to be aware of possible influences on rating responses due to specific characteristics of the course, of students, or of teachers—characteristics that have little to do with actual teacher or course effectiveness. Most extraneous variables have a relatively weak relationship to ratings. But a few—small classes, for example—seem to get higher ratings and are generally advantageous. Such characteristics should be considered in interpreting results.

7. Standardized procedures in administering forms are recommended if the results are to be used in personnel decisions. One method is to have a student or someone other than the teacher distribute, collect, and place the questionnaires in a sealed envelope, the teacher not being present during the process. The timing—preferably during the last week or two of class—should also be standard. Mailing the forms to students usually results in a poor response rate.

THREE

Benefits of Self-Assessment and Self-Analysis

Teacher self-evaluation or self-reports are generally minor factors in tenure and promotion evaluations. The department chairmen surveyed by Centra (1977a) ranked self-evaluation as ninth among fifteen criteria, and few department chairmen gave them more importance than that. Other studies concur. According to Larson (1970), fewer than 10 percent of the English department chairmen surveyed by him collected written self-evaluations. Seldin (1978) reports that about 20 percent of the liberal arts college deans in his 1973 study used self-evaluation, but by 1978 the number reached 36 percent, indicating that the use of self-assessment or self-reports in tenure and promotion decisions is increasing among some colleges.

What Is Meant by Self-Assessment?

Narrowly defined, in self-assessment teachers rate their effectiveness on a scaled form or provide brief written evaluations of their teaching performance. Such information is not generally as useful for tenure and promotion purposes as the descriptions or reports of teaching and other activities provided by the faculty member at the end of each year. While the latter may include the teachers' judgments of their effectiveness, their purpose is to report the details of teaching, research, and other tangible evidence of accomplishment. The emphasis is on description rather than assessment. Colleges that report increasing use of self-evaluation or self-reports may be referring to this descriptive information.

The goal of self-analysis is to encourage the teacher to examine closely what he or she is doing by answering a series of probing questions regarding teaching methods or by viewing video or audio replays of their classes. Self-analysis is especially important in developing a professional and personal growth plan because it depends on an accurate scrutiny of one's strengths and weaknesses.

What Does Research Say About Self-Evaluation?

Several recent studies support the use of self-assessment procedures as a way of helping to focus a teacher's attention on performance. Combined with other evaluative procedures, self-evaluation can be particularly useful in a nonthreatening situation. But for many teachers who have an inflated view of their performance, a view that might become even more inflated or defensive if their assessments were used administratively, self-evaluations are of little use in making tenure, promotion, and salary decisions.

The study of 343 teaching faculty from five colleges conducted by Centra in 1973(b) compared self-ratings with student ratings of college teachers on twenty-one items dealing with instructional practices. Teacher self-ratings had only a modest relationship with student ratings (a median correlation of .21). In addition to this general lack of agreement, some 30 percent of the teachers gave themselves better ratings than did their students, while an average of 6 percent of the teachers gave themselves considerably poorer ratings. In a sense, the better ratings might be viewed as only "human"; Robert Burns reminds us that most people do not see themselves as others see them. Another point to consider: teachers in this study were assured that only they would see the rating results. If they knew that ratings were to be used in determining promotions, self-ratings would probably be higher and the difference from student ratings even greater.

Although these findings indicate that self-ratings should be used cautiously in tenure, promotion, and salary deliberations, other analyses find them useful for teaching improvement. A ranking of item mean responses for the teacher and student groups shows that both tend to see the same relative strengths and weaknesses among teachers. The rank correlation of .77 indicates fairly high similarity in the way both groups ordered the items (Centra, 1973b; Marsh, Overall, and Kesler, 1978), showing that teachers are apparently able to identify their stronger and weaker points—even though they use only the positive end of a scale in doing so. They also have a good idea of which are their best courses. Marsh, Overall, and Kesler asked faculty to indicate their "most effective" and "least effective" course; the student assessments of courses that the faculty identified as most effective were higher on all evaluation dimensions. Teaching consultants working with individual teachers may therefore find it useful to combine an "ipsative" assessment approach (in which teachers make comparisons among their own various teaching practices) with a "normative" approach (in which teacher ratings or "scores" on each practice are compared with those of other teachers). A specific ipsative self-rating instrument will be discussed later in this chapter.

That self-ratings correlate poorly with student ratings is also shown by Choy (1969) and Blackburn and Clark (1975). The latter, moreover, find that although colleague and administrator ratings do not agree with self-ratings, they agree substantially with each other as well as with student ratings. Self-ratings, in short, were the only set Blackburn and Clark found to be dissimilar. A few studies, however, report a significant positive relationship between self-ratings and student ratings. Webb and Nolan (1955), in a military setting, found the highest correlation—.62 for fifty-one instructors. Two studies in academic settings show correlations between self-ratings and student ratings as .47 for fourteen teaching assistants (Doyle and Crichton, 1978) and .49 for fifty-one social science faculty members (Marsh,

Overall, and Kesler, 1978). A reason for this closer agreement may be that the instructors were previously rated by students and had lowered their self-ratings as a result. In Centra (1973b), most of the faculty members in the five participating colleges had not previously collected student ratings from their classes—which was why those particular colleges were chosen. The Braskamp and Caulley (1978) study supports this view. By collecting self-ratings and student ratings in successive semesters for the same group of teachers, they found that the two converged during the second semester because of the teachers' lowered self-ratings.

Self-ratings do not appear to be distorted by known instructor characteristics such as sex, age, tenure status, teaching load, or years of experience (Doyle and Webber, 1978). Measured intelligence and the amount of formal education received by a teacher are also unrelated to self-ratings, at least as indicated by Webb and Nolan's study (1955) of Air Force instructors.

Some Approaches to Self-Analysis

Quakers and other groups use a self-analysis or self-questioning technique to help individuals examine their conduct and performance. Might a similar approach be useful to faculty members to improve their teaching? Boulding (1970, pp. 119–121) thinks so. He proposes a list of "queries" that teachers might use in examining their practices. Included are:

- Do I abuse my position of superior status to the student by treating him as a moral or social inferior? (Boulding adds that we need to know the extent to which bullying and sarcasm are blocks to learning, as well as the effects of emphasizing equality of status between teacher and student.)
- Am I careful to avoid using my authority to force factual acceptance of propositions which may be only opinion or hypothesis? Do I tolerate honest disagreement?
- Do I express my covert or overt hostility to my students in my teaching? Am I irritated by student failure, or am I quick to detect and encourage growth in knowledge and understanding, however slow or imperfect?

- Am I myself interested in the subject matter that I am teaching? Do I enjoy learning more about it, and do I carry over to the student my own enthusiasm for the subject?
- Do I convey to my students both the setting and the significance of my subject matter, so that it is neither isolated nor irrelevant?

Boulding, then, thinks that teachers need to guard against being authoritarian, hostile, close-minded, unenthusiastic, or irrelevant. Undoubtedly it would be possible to formulate a set of queries based on other general characteristics. For example, the "Form for Faculty Self Evaluation" (Exhibit 8; Larson, 1970) states that an instructor should "maintain a high level of enthusiasm and excitement about the positive value of learning," although its questions go beyond these traits by having teachers evaluate such things as their use of tests and grading. Needed in addition are developmental activities for teachers. The "Self-Appraisal Form for Faculty" (Exhibit 9) developed by the Faculty and Instructional Development Office of San Jose State University is tied into such activities; materials and activities are designed to help individuals in each of the general areas on the form. Thus workbook and workshop suggestions are available to help faculty improve testing procedures, discussion techniques, instructional/student relationships, and other aspects of teaching. In some categories, assistance can vary from the traditional to the innovative. In the "Instructional Strategies" category, for example, teachers may see the need to simply improve the organization of their lectures or they may want to adopt a self-paced learning approach in a course. Materials and assistance from the Faculty and Instructional Development Office are available for either alternative.

Like the San Jose form, the Instructor Self-Evaluation Form (ISEF) developed at the University of Illinois is designed as a catalyst to help teachers rectify their weaknesses (Batista and Brandenburg, in press). ISEF provides instructors with scores on four subscales: "adequacy of classroom procedures, enthusiasm and knowledge for teaching," "stimulation of cognitive and affective gains in students," and "relations with students." Instructors respond to a series of items listed in sets of four by ranking each item from the most to the least descriptive of their teaching. For example: "a. I present ideas clearly," "b. I enjoy teaching my own course," "c. I stimulate

Exhibit 8. A Form for Faculty Self-Evaluation

Excellence in teaching, as defined in our faculty handbook, is that which will inspire and convey the *excitement* of learning. This would seem to imply a necessity for the instructor to maintain a high level of enthusiasm and excitement about the positive value of learning. With this requirement in mind, the following questions seem appropriate to ask of ourselves.

1. AL=ALWAYS   2. US=USUALLY   3. SM=SELDOM
4. NV=NEVER   5. DK=DON'T KNOW
Circle the appropriate response.

A. Preparation—Do I
   1. Keep up with the current literature
      in my field?   AL   US   SM   NV   DK
   2. Attend workshops and conventions?   AL   US   SM   NV   DK
   3. Update class presentations with new
      information?   AL   US   SM   NV   DK
   4. Seek better textbooks and materials
      often?   AL   US   SM   NV   DK
B. Class—Do I
   1. Know, to the best of my ability, who
      my students are—names, ability,
      and background?   AL   US   SM   NV   DK
   2. Try to design class to meet needs of
      all student levels of experience?   AL   US   SM   NV   DK
   3. Leave the class anticipating with
      pleasure the next meeting?   AL   US   SM   NV   DK
   4. Let students know clearly my
      expectations of them?   AL   US   SM   NV   DK
   5. Encourage and/or insist on questions
      and discussion?   AL   US   SM   NV   DK
   6. Give tests which evaluate how well
      my stated goals have been reached?   AL   US   SM   NV   DK
   7. Remain an impartial and fair
      evaluator?   AL   US   SM   NV   DK
   8. Invite a failing student in for
      conferences?   AL   US   SM   NV   DK
   9. Change my methods when students
      seem not to be learning?   AL   US   SM   NV   DK
  10. Explain exactly how final grades
      are derived?   AL   US   SM   NV   DK
  11. Keep accurate and efficient records to
      show students who wish grade
      reviewed?   AL   US   SM   NV   DK
  12. Return papers promptly and marked so
      students can see what they did right?   AL   US   SM   NV   DK
  13. Use tests as a teaching device?   AL   US   SM   NV   DK
  14. Avoid using the same tests from
      year to year?   AL   US   SM   NV   DK

Exhibit 8. (continued)

15. Make different tests of equal difficulty
for each section of the same course?   AL US SM NV DK
16. Maintain office hours regularly during
which students may drop in or
schedule conferences?   AL US SM NV DK
17. Perceive students as individuals instead
of stereotyping?   AL US SM NV DK
18. Try to find loopholes in my teaching
and correct them?   AL US SM NV DK
19. Use books and library assignments to
enrich classroom instruction?   AL US SM NV DK
20. Encourage independent reading as a
lifetime habit for my students?   AL US SM NV DK
21. Set an example for my students by
referring to books in my class lectures
and discussions?   AL US SM NV DK

Source: Larson (1970).

Exhibit 9. A Self-Appraisal Form for Faculty

The basic purpose of this form is to help you identify professional areas you would like to further develop. The Faculty and Instructional Development Office has assembled various resources and activities which may assist you in meeting the needs you have identified.

Below are listed five major instructional areas. Please read the descriptions under each area and circle the appropriate response(s) for each description.

A   Not Necessary—I don't feel that I need help in this area.
B   Low Priority—I am interested, but for the time being, this is a low priority.
C   More Information—I'd like to find out more about this area.
D   Ready for Action—I would like to become involved in this area *as soon as possible.*

Instructional Strategies: (Lectures, Self-Paced Learning, etc.)

A B C D   Give effective lectures with clear goals, appropriate examples, and in a well-organized manner.

A B C D   Make use of a variety of media and resources in my instruction to add interest and clarity.

A B C D   Provide opportunities for independent study and small group work through planned modules and support resources.

A B C D   Design an instructional system in which the students are pretested and guided into alternative activities (self-paced and group) to reach desired learning outcomes.

Exhibit 9. (continued)

Tests and Evaluation of Learning:

A B C D   Use assessment techniques to measure the student's knowledge of the course content, based on my standards from previous semesters.

A B C D   Use assessment techniques to measure the student's understanding and ability to apply his knowledge.

A B C D   Use assessment techniques to measure the student's levels of knowledge, ability to apply intellectual skills, and develop attitudes toward further learning.

A B C D   Use assessment techniques to measure the student's competency to use knowledge and intellectual skills for analysis and problem solving.

Discussion Techniques:

A B C D   Have students respond to questions I raise.

A B C D   Have students develop and ask me questions related to the topic.

A B C D   Have students raise questions to develop a free inter-action within the group.

A B C D   Have an exchange with and among the students so that both the students and I measurably benefit.

Instructor/Student Relationship:

A B C D   Establish an atmosphere in the classroom so that the students will be receptive to the instructional program.

A B C D   Build good rapport with the students in order to ascertain and meet their needs.

A B C D   Develop sound interpersonal relationships with students in order to encourage their personal development and self-confidence.

A B C D   Create a common ground with students in order to collaborate with them in realistic problem solving activities.

Course Structure:

A B C D   Plan my course in order to present the subject matter in a well-structured and logical manner.

A B C D   Provide flexibility in course structure by relating it to the self-perceived needs of the students.

A B C D   Develop the course based on a specified set of performance objectives and provide alternative means for the students to reach to objectives.

A B C D   Develop a course in a systematic way and, in addition to providing alternatives to students, I obtain their feedback for course restructuring and improvement.

For information or assistance regarding areas you have identified, contact the Faculty and Instructional Development Office (Ron McBeath or Jerry Kemp, at 7-3411/7-3413). We will be pleased to discuss ways to help you in reaching your objectives.

Source: This form has been developed and is being validated by the Faculty and Instructional Development Office of San Jose State University. Copyright 1976.

students' interest in the subject," and "d. I am fair and impartial in dealing with students." The instructors then indicate which item is the most descriptive and which is the least descriptive. Items in each set were matched on desirability. This forced-choice approach results in a relative positioning of the four teaching dimensions within each person (ipsative scores), thus identifying what teachers see as their own relative strengths and weaknesses. A drawback to the approach, however, is that some teachers who may actually be weak in *several* areas would not know this from the ISEF results.

The queries and instruments discussed are most useful with conscientious and open teachers; such a mild form of confrontation may be all some teachers need to seek ways of improving themselves. But for other teachers, particularly those who most need to improve, a stronger form of self-confrontation is needed. That confrontation may come through audio or video playback.

Does Tape Playback Help?

Video playback has been used for training or therapy with such populations as athletes, salesmen, alcoholics, and preservice teachers. With its increased availability, video equipment is being used by full-time faculty and teaching assistants in many colleges and universities. Of the 756 institutions that replied to the Centra (1976a) survey of faculty development practices, 57 percent had video equipment available for instructional improvement. At most of these institutions, however, fewer than 5 percent actually used video playback, perhaps due to its disruptive and threatening effect on some faculty members.

Fuller and Manning (1973), after reviewing over 300 studies, concluded that self-confrontation through video playback has the potential to help and to harm. Few of these studies were conducted with college teachers, but many of their findings could be generalized. When teachers are required to submit to video playback against their strong objection or if they have disabilities that cannot be remedied, deleterious effects are most likely. A change in teaching behavior is much more likely when a peer or a teaching counselor analyzes or "focuses" the playback.

Viewing and analyzing the playback alone is less threatening, but seems to produce desirable changes only when teachers can compare their performance with a model of "good teaching" or with some desired standards (Salomon and McDonald, 1970), an indication that guide sheets may help teachers to appraise their own video playbacks. They may draw attention to more than the surprising sound of the teacher's voice or to an unusual mannerism. Viewing the playback with someone else—particularly someone with the appropriate expertise—can help to identify discrepancies between desired and actual performance. Remedial action can also be offered. Kindsvatter and Wilen (1977) devised a set of observational instruments to help the individual teacher and/or an observer focus on specific critical behaviors. Three of the instruments, Exhibits 10, 11, and 12, cover the instructional skill areas of "questions and questioning," "lecture," and "recitation and discussion."

Videotaping is an important part of the minicourse program, a training device used to help elementary school teachers master instructional skills (Borg and others, 1970). The program includes modeling (watching model teachers perform specific skills) and microteaching. A videotape is made by students in a short demonstration lesson, the tape is evaluated by a student and an observer, and the lesson is retaught. Research evidence is positive regarding the value of the minicourse technique in improving such instructional skills as question-phrasing (Borg, 1972). This approach may adapt itself for use with graduate teaching assistants.

How Does Audio Compare with Video Playback? Listening to one's own voice on a tape, Fuller and Manning (1973) conclude, is like "being given a little shake, but self-viewing is like a teethrattling blow." Although audio is less threatening, it is also less motivating; this may explain why it is far less used than videotaping. Fuller and Manning suggest combining audio and video by using video playback initially and switching to audio playback for long-term practice toward improvement. Most people can "visualize" what is going on from the audio alone. Such a procedure provides for the continued flow of information essential for improvement, but in a relatively inexpensive and simple manner.

Tape playbacks, both visual and audio, are most useful for instructional improvement and are a potential help in making tenure

Exhibit 10. Analysis of Instruction: Questions and Questioning

Questioning is considered one of the most influential teaching acts because it is the most basic way by which a teacher stimulates student learning and thinking. In order to achieve objectives at varying cognitive levels, teachers need to employ instructional strategies that incorporate questions congruent to the level of thinking desired. For example, recitation and some guided discovery strategies are best accomplished by using lower-level closed questions; whereas the inquiry approach necessitates the use of higher-level open-ended questions. Teachers need to strive for a balance between questions that require the recall of information and questions that require critical thinking.

The formation of questions appropriate to desired objectives is extremely important, but no more so than the questioning process. The teacher's effectiveness as a questioner depends not only on devising good questions but also on the way questions are asked. Effectively phrased questions help to focus the thrust of learning, and promote thoughtfulness in the student's responses.

Questions: Cognitive Levels

The following classification scheme for cognitive levels of questions is based on Aschner and Gallagher's well-known adaptation of Guilford's "structure of the intellect" model.

1. *Cognitive-Memory Questions:* The teacher's intention is having students recall or recognize information. Cognitive-memory questions are narrow, closed questions that require the lowest level of thinking and the students' responses can be anticipated. A student responds to a cognitive-memory question by performing such behaviors as recalling specific facts, defining, recounting, repeating, answering "yes" or "no," quoting, or identifying what has been observed. Some examples are: "What did you observe in this experiment?" "What is the quadratic formula?" "How do you spell 'photosynthesis,' John?" "Did the U.S. pay $15 million for the Louisiana Territory?" "What is an epic?"

2. *Convergent Questions:* The teacher's intention is having students analyze and combine given or remembered information. Convergent questions are also narrow, closed questions, but require higher-level thinking and are less restricted than cognitive-memory questions. The answers to this kind of question are generally predictable. A student responds to a convergent question by performing such behaviors as translating, interpreting, relating, comparing, contrasting, explaining, associating, concluding, and summarizing data and information. Some examples are: "How are Jacksonian and Jeffersonian Democracy similar?" "What conclusions can you come up with?" "In your own words, what influence did James Baldwin's works have on the Black Movement?" "What does this graph tell you regarding population trends?" "How would you translate this sentence into German?" "How does the use of the slide rule compare with the calculator?"

Exhibit 10. (continued)

3. *Divergent Questions:* The teacher's intention is having students independently develop their own information or view a given topic from a new perspective. Divergent questions are broad, open-ended questions because they permit a variety of responses. The answers to this type of question are thought-provoking, original, and generally cannot be anticipated. These questions are often associated with creative thinking. A student responds to a divergent question by performing such behaviors as hypothesizing, speculating, predicting, implying, synthesizing, inferring, devising plans and solving problems. Some examples are: "How might you go about gathering information on this problem?" "What predictions can you make about the future of the UN?" "How would you design a building to accommodate all these features?" "Supposing Cezanne were alive today, how would he react to these paintings?"

4. *Evaluative Questions:* The teacher's intention is having students project and support their judgments, values, and choices. Evaluative questions represent the highest level of questioning and, for the most part, involve the use of cognitive operations from all the other levels. They are also broad, open-ended questions because of the diversity and unpredictability of responses. A student responds to this type of question by performing such behaviors as judging, valuing, choosing, rating, and offering opinions. After a student has taken a self-selected position, he should support or defend his position by using internal or external standards. Some examples are: "Are you for or against abortion?" "Do you think this should be considered a great work of art?" "What recording group is your favorite?" "Which condition would you have preferred, working for the CCC or receiving unemployment compensation?" "What do you think of John Jones as a Vice-Presidential candidate?" Examples of follow-up questions to initial evaluative level questions include: "Can you support your opinion?" "Why do you think that?" "What evidence do you have?"

Questoning: Phrasing

1. *Appropriate Question Level:* Provide a balance between closed (cognitive-memory and convergent) and open-ended (divergent and evaluative) questions. Research shows that 60–70% of teachers' questions require low-level thinking. Higher-level thinking is also important in order for students to use the knowledge they have learned.

2. *Allow Thinking Time:* Provide sufficient pauses after asking divergent and evaluative level questions. Questions at these levels require more time and reflection for students to formulate thoughtful responses.

3. *Group-Individual Balance:* Provide a balance between group-oriented and individual student questions. Group-oriented questions broaden class participation while individual questions can be used to get students to extend initial responses and involve stduents who normally do not participate in discussions. The balance provides a variation in approach and keeps students actively involved.

Exhibit 10. (continued)

4. *Participation:* Provide a balance in participation by calling on both volunteering and nonvolunteering students. Often only a few students participate, and therefore dominate classroom discussions. Encouraging reticent students to participate can be rewarding to both student and teacher.

5. Follow-Up Questions: Follow-up initial student responses, when appropriate, with questions that encourage them to complete, clarify, expand, or support answers. This technique encourages students to extend their thinking beyond an initial (and sometimes superficial) response.

6. *Appropriate Verbal Level:* Phrase questions according to the language and ability level of the students. This helps decrease anxiety and frustration, and promotes understanding—all of which are requisites to effective learning.

Self-Analysis or Shared-Analysis of Performance

This instrument can be employed in at least three ways for use in instructional analysis. The most effective outcome occurs if the instrument is used by the teacher and observer in conjunction with a video or audio tape recording of the teaching episode. For self-analysis (no observer present) the instrument aids in focusing the teacher's attention on specific pertinent behaviors as he views the video tape (or hears the audio tape) alone. When a tape recorder isn't available, an observer can use the instrument to record impressions to share with the teacher.

Before teaching the lesson:
1. What teaching method will I use to achieve my objectives?

2. What approximate mix of closed- and open-ended questions do I anticipate using?

3. What are some examples of the questions I intend to ask in class (especially crucial when higher-level student thinking is intended)?

After teaching the lesson:
1. To what extent did I achieve my objectives?

2. Were the questions appropriate for the instructional strategy utilized?

3. Did I come sufficiently close to the mix anticipated?

4. In what ways was student participation affected by the use of the kinds of questions I asked?

5. If I had the opportunity to teach the lesson over, in what ways would I change my approach to questioning the students?

6. How can I continue to improve in formulating and expressing questions?

Exhibit 10. (continued)

Analysis Scales

		Extent	Appraisal
Teacher	_____	1. Not evident	1. Not competent
Observer	_____	2. Slightly evident	2. Slightly competent
		3. Moderately evident	3. Moderately competent
Class	_____	4. Quite evident	4. Quite competent
Date	_____	N Not applicable	N Not apꞁ 'icable

Extent   *Appraisal*

Phrasing:
1. Appropriate Question Level: teacher used questions at appropriate levels to achieve the objectives of the lesson.   _____ _____
2. Allows Thinking Time: teacher paused sufficiently after asking higher-level questions in order to allow student thinking.   _____ _____
3. Group-Individual Balance: teacher provided a balance between group-oriented and individual student questions.   _____ _____
4. Participation: teacher encouraged participation by calling on volunteers and nonvolunteers.   _____ _____
5. Follow-up Questions: teacher followed up initial student responses with questions that encouraged students to complete, clarify, expand, or support.   _____ _____
6. Appropriate Verbal Level: teacher adjusted questions to the language and ability level of the students.   _____ _____

*No. of
Questions   Est. Percent
Asked   of Total*

Cognitive Levels:
1. Cognitive-Memory: narrow, closed questions that require students to recall or recognize information. Students recognized, recalled, defined, recounted, repeated, quoted, identified, or answered "yes" or "no."   _____ _____
2. Convergent: narrow questions that require students to analyze and combine remembered information. Students translated, interpreted, related, explained, compared, contrasted, analyzed, associated, concluded, or summarized.   _____ _____

Exhibit 10. (continued)

3. Divergent: broad, open-ended questions that require students to develop their own information or to view a topic from a new perspective. Students hypothesized, speculated,
devised, inferred, predicted, implied, syn-
thesized, or solved.   _____   _____
4. Evaluative: broad, open-ended questions that
require students to judge, value, or choose
with support from internal or external
sources. Students opined, judged, rated per
an explicit criterion, or made and defended
a choice.   _____   _____

Total Number of Questions Asked _____

Exhibit 11. Analysis of Instruction: Lecture

The lecture is the most traditional and, considering all its forms, the
mostly widely used approach to instruction. It is also the most criticized
because of its teacher-centered nature and general misuse at all levels of
education. The type of lecture can range from a formal extended presentation,
used primarily in high school and college large-group sessions, to informal
explanations used at both elementary and secondary levels. A major
characteristic of all lectures, though, is that the teacher engages primarily in
one-way communication and thus dominates classroom verbal activity.
Although the time period of a lecture may range from several minutes to over
an hour, the students' role is mainly a passive one with 80–90 percent of the
verbalizations being teacher-talk.

The vast majority of lectures are used for the purposes of introducing,
informing, explaining, demonstrating, and summarizing. Another very
beneficial use of the lecture is to stimulate students' critical thinking skills by
presenting a problematic area with the intention that follow-up inquiry will
be fostered in smaller discussion groups. It is at this time that the students
assume an active role as learners. The most effective use of the lecture occurs
when it serves as a springboard to further inquiry and when it complements a
variety of other instructional approaches.

Components of the Lecture

1. *Entry:* Introduce the lecture in an interesting and original way so as to
focus attention immediately on the topic or problematic area. Entry not only
serves to "grab" the attention of the audience but also to provide advanced
organizers so that the audience fully understands the purpose and structure of
the lecture. In order to clearly communicate intent, objectives and/or an
outline of major points may be exhibited or distributed to the students.

2. *Content:* The emphasis of the lecture must be on the broader concepts,
principles, and generalizations rather than upon specific facts. A major goal

Exhibit 11. (continued)

of the lecture is to stimulate the audience intellectually. This can best be achieved when the relationship and application of knowledge are presented rather than the facts themselves. Specific facts should be used to support generalizations, hypotheses, principles, theories, and problems, not as ends in themselves.

3. *Presentation:* The lecturer should present his remarks in an enthusiastic manner throughout the exposition so as to hold audience attention. Particular attention must be paid to facial expressions and hand and body gestures to emphasize the major points, voice volume and tone to maintain a vibrant delivery, and eye contact with the audience to attempt to personally involve individuals.

4. *Audio-Visual Aids:* In order to organize, clarify, and illustrate major themes in the presentation, audio-visual aids or other props should be used. Care must be taken to insure that the aids complement the lecture rather than serve as a substitute.

5. *Participation:* Consideration must be given to the involvement of the student audience either during or immediately after the lecture. In the case of the informal lecture it would be appropriate for the lecturer to ask questions during the presentation and encourage students to ask questions and make comments. During the extended lecture, though, student questions should be reserved until the end of the presentation because of the highly structured framework within which the lecturer delivers. Active student involvement, in one way or another, must remain the most important component of any instructional approach and it must be accommodated.

6. *Closure:* Lecture closure must center around providing a summary of the major points presented and a springboard to the follow-up activity. The summary assists the audience in comprehending the broader conceptualization of the topic or problem by focusing on the important components. The springboard serves as the charge or challenge for the students to pursue in smaller discussion groups in the case of the extended lecture. For example, if the lecture centered around stimulating student awareness and comprehension of a persisting social problem, the springboard could be delivered in the form of thought-provoking questions for the students to consider as a basis for active inquiry.

Self-Analysis or Shared-Analysis of Performance

This instrument can be employed in at least three ways for use in instructional analysis. The most effective outcome occurs if the instrument is used by the teacher and observer in conjunction with a video or audio tape recording of the teaching episode. For self-analysis (no observer present) the instrument aids in focusing the teacher's attention on specific pertinent behaviors as he views the video tape (or hears the audio tape) alone. When a tape recorder isn't available, an observer can use the instrument to record impressions to share with the teacher.

Exhibit 11. (continued)

Before teaching the lesson:

1. How will the use of the lecture approach help achieve my objectives?

2. What questions have I planned to involve the student audience either during or immediately after the presentation?

3. In what ways will I monitor my verbal and nonverbal behaviors and audience reaction so as to ensure an enthusiastic presentation?

4. Have I rehearsed the presentation sufficiently taking into account the time factor and the smooth incorporation of audio-visual aids (in the case of an extended lecture)?

After teaching the lesson:

1. To what extent were my objectives achieved?

2. What specific clues did the audience display as indicators of how well the lecture was received?

3. If I had the opportunity to deliver the lecture again, in what ways would I alter my approach to the students?

Analysis Scales

	Extent	Appraisal
Teacher _____	1. Not evident	1. Not competent
Observer _____	2. Slightly evident	2. Slightly competent
	3. Moderately evident	3. Moderately competent
Class _____	4. Quite evident	4. Quite competent
Date _____	N Not applicable	N Not applicable

	Extent	Appraisal
1. Entry: The lecture was introduced in an interesting way and the purpose and structure of the lecture were clearly communicated.	_____	_____
2. Content: emphasis was on presenting concepts, principles, generalizations, and other forms of broad knowledge. The audience was stimulated intellectually.	_____	_____
3. Presentation: the lecture was presented in a vibrant and lively manner. Use of gestures, variation in voice volume and tone, and eye contact with audience were evident.	_____	_____
4. Audio-Visual Aids: audio-visual aids were used to organize, clarify, or illustrate major points.	_____	_____

Exhibit 11. (continued)

5. Participation: audience was encouraged to become involved by asking questions or making comments during or after the lecture.   _____   _____
6. Closure: a summary of the major points stressed was provided and a springboard to conduct further inquiry was included.   _____   _____

Exhibit 12. Analysis of Instruction: Recitation and Discussion

A sizeable proportion of the learning activity in most classrooms is made up of teacher-student verbal interaction. In fact, the most typical image of the teacher is that of a person involved in verbal interaction with students. One can hardly conceive of a classroom, other than a laboratory setting or a highly programmed situation, in which verbal interaction doesn't occur to a considerable extent. In other words, recitation and discussion are nearly pervasive to teaching, and are essential to the style of education that is prevalent in American schools.

Recitation

Verbal interaction in the classroom is usually referred to as discussion. Technically, most of what we describe as discussion is actually recitation. It is usually characterized by: (1) a fairly tightly structured situation, with the teacher firmly in control of proceedings; (2) the desks arranged in rows with the teacher in front; (3) many teacher questions interspersed with brief teacher comments (short of lecture); (4) necessary but restricted student involvement; (5) the covering of a predetermined segment of subject matter; (6) emphasis on lower levels of student thought.

Recitation tends to be the method that teachers adopt—or resort to—almost intuitively, or at least without due consideration. Instead, the use of recitation should follow a deliberate decision that this is the most effective means available to achieve the immediate objectives.

Recitation can be an effective method for achieving certain classroom objectives, although it is probably over-used. It is useful, e.g., as a means of clarifying information following a reading assignment, lecture, film, or combined with lecture. On the other hand, recitation is less useful than certain other techniques for helping students discover personal meanings. In practice, recitation usually, but not exclusively, involves primarily memory-level thinking; it is less likely to demand divergent-level thinking. Nor does it, as generally employed, require students to consider and question attitudes and values. So, while recitation under the direction of a skillful teacher may involve thinking at any level, and while it surely contributes to effective teaching when selectively employed, its limitations should be recognized.

Exhibit 12. (continued)

The limitations are related to the restricted extent of student "freedom" in the recitation setting as compared to discussion and certain other methods.

Discussion

Actual cases of discussion in the classroom are more rare than most teachers realize. On the other hand, there are instances in which elements of discussion occur within a recitation in such a way that is difficult to discern which is the predominant mode at a given time. It is not especially important to distinguish at any moment which mode is being employed; it is more important to note the quality of the interaction that is occurring.

Discussion, when it occurs, is characterized by: (1) the recognition by the students of an issue or problem upon which their attention is focused; (2) an attempt by the students to reach consensus on the issue or a solution to the problem; (3) a considerable degree of freedom of the students in their verbal interaction; (4) the role of the teacher as more supportive than dominative; (5) emphasis on higher levels of thought.

Discussion is particularly appropriate as a means of helping students deal with situations involving their attitudes and values. However, any classroom topic that can be posed as an issue or problem has the potential to be the basis for a meaningful discussion. Some courses such as social studies, humanities, and health offer numerous possibilities for discussion. Other more structured courses, such as foreign language, mathematics, and chemistry are less likely settings for discussion.

Self-Analysis or Shared-Analysis of Performance

This instrument can be employed in at least three ways for use in instructional analysis. The most effective outcome of the instrument is used by the teacher and observer in conjunction with a video tape recording of the teaching episode. For self-analysis (no observer present) the instrument aids in focusing the teacher's attention on specific pertinent behaviors as he views the video tape (or hears the audio tape) alone. When a video tape recorder isn't available, an observer can use the instrument to record impressions to share with the teacher.

Before teaching the lesson:
1. What do I intend to be the learning outcomes of this lesson?

2. If I am employing recitation, what segment of subject matter do I plan to cover; if a discussion, what is the immediate issue or problem?

3. What is the rationale for employing recitation or discussion as the primary strategy?

Exhibit 12. (continued)

After teaching the lesson:

1. To what extent were my planned learning outcomes achieved?

2. On the whole, do I feel I conducted the recitation or discussion competently?

3. What suggestions do I have for improving a similar lesson in the future?

Analysis Scales

	Extent	*Appraisal*
Teacher _____	1. Not evident	1. Not competent
Observer _____	2. Slightly evident	2. Slightly competent
Class _____	3. Moderately evident	3. Moderately competent
	4. Quite evident	4. Quite competent
Date _____	N Not applicable	N Not applicable

Extent   *Appraisal*

1. Organizing Scheme: an explicit objective(s) is a reference point; or a particular theme or focus is apparent.
2. Articulate Teacher Commentary: teacher contributions keep to the point, arouse students' interest, provide appropriate elaboration and continuity, but are not protracted.   _____   _____
3. Competency in Questioning: questions are incisively stated, their intent is clear; questions vary to include both convergent and divergent thinking; a questioning pattern or strategy is apparent.   _____   _____
4. Teacher Listening: the teacher hears the students out with minimum interruption; the teacher indicates attention and encouragement through nonverbal expression.   _____   _____
5. Respectful Climate: courtesy characterizes verbal interaction; students' right to speak and be heard is protected; teacher deals decisively with rude or inconsiderate behavior.   _____   _____
6. Clarification and Summarization: the teacher analyzes or restates when there is a possibility of misunderstanding; the teacher pulls together ideas when necessary to facilitate understanding.   _____   _____
7. Reinforcing Behavior: the teacher responds to student contributions in a supportive and encouraging way; students are frequently commended, criticism is kept at a minimum; the teacher accepts and uses students' ideas.   _____   _____
8. Student Involvement: many different students make verbal contributions; many student comments reflect the students' own ideas.   _____   _____

Exhibit 12. (continued)

Recitation Only:

1. Deliberate Development of Topic: the teacher employs commentary and questions systematically in pursuing the learning objective; the class stays "on track."   _____ _____

Discussion Only:

1. Issue or Problem Orientation: the discussion relates to a real issue or a meaningful problem.   _____ _____
2. Student Initiative: the center of action shifts from the teacher to the students; there is student-to-student talk; students accept responsibility.   _____ _____
3. Democratic Process: the class seeks consensus as the outcome of discussion; opposing views are given a full hearing; the teacher is largely a resource person.   _____ _____

and promotion decisions. Faculty members can submit selected tapes to be viewed by administrators and evaluation committees; video is more informative than audio, since the reactions of students in the class can also be noted. Video recordings from several courses are fairly representative of a teacher's performance.

Individualized Development Plans or Growth Contracts

Self-analysis is a key element in growth contracting. This approach calls for faculty members, administrators, and the staff to set goals for themselves that they hope to accomplish in a given period of time—usually one year. Identifying one's strengths and weaknesses is an important first step, followed by periodic meetings with a dean or colleague to discuss the contract and to assess progress toward each specified goal. The plan has several variations. At Austin College in Texas, every faculty member, tenured or not, develops a negotiated career plan at four-year intervals. At the end of each academic year the teacher and an associate dean discuss the degree of success attained for each specified objective, consider evaluation plans and results, and review progress toward the long-range goals. The college covers expenses incurred in self-renewal activities.

At New College, part of the University of Alabama, all members of the faculty and staff, clerical and secretarial included, draw up annual growth contracts including personal and professional goals. The contract, however, is not in any way used to make promotion, salary, and tenure decisions. The college believes this is necessary to ensure that the staff will be honest in identifying weaknesses and seeking their solution. Growth contracts are related to the institutional reward system at Gordon College in Massachusetts. An evaluation committee that is in part selected by the faculty member assesses progress toward the instructor's goals. (See Smith, 1976, for more detail on the Gordon and New College procedures.)

It makes good sense to appraise the content of a growth contract as well as the progress made toward its objectives. The administrative use of this information rewards staff members for their present effectiveness, a primary aim, and for their progress in self-renewal. Faculty members often need help in designing a suitable plan; otherwise, their plans may become simply listings of conferences that they would like to attend, trips that they want to take, and the like.

Concluding Recommendation: What Information Should Instructors Provide?

Although self-ratings are not especially valid, a summative evaluation should focus on an accurate description of a faculty member's teaching, research, and other activities. Lists of research articles, books, proposals, committees, and out-of-class activities are fairly straightforward, but a description of teaching is more complex. Beyond such basic information as the number of courses and students taught, teachers should provide evidence concerning such a wide range of questions as the following, an expansion of some offered by McIntyre (1977):

1. *Instructor objectives and activities:* What was the instructor trying to accomplish in the course and what techniques or strategies were used? Were new approaches being tried? Is there evidence of how well they worked? Were there outcomes or circumstances that would not be noticed in other evaluation data collected about the teacher? Did the teacher's objectives for the course fit in with the department and college curricula? To what extent did the

Exhibit 13. Example of a Faculty Growth Contract

Joe Doaks—Assistant Professor of Biology
Contract Period—September, 1979–August, 1981

I. Self-assessment
   A. Strengths
      1. Design and supervision of laboratory work.
      2. Interest and ability in advising students in a one-to-one relationship.
      3. Research skills and background.
      4. Interdisciplinary interest and knowledge.
      5. Fairly broad bibliographic background in most areas of Natural Science and Mathematics.
   B. Weaknesses
      1. Lecturing ability, particularly in larger classes.
      2. General laziness in writing up my research for publication.
      3. Lack of experience in scientific work in other than an academic setting.
      4. Minimal contact with students outside the classroom, laboratory, and office.
      5. An inability to construct good examinations except in laboratories.

II. Areas of contribution and means of evaluation
   A. Teach upper-division, research, and seminar courses as indicated in the catalog.
      1. Student evaluation forms will be administered in each class, the results discussed with the department head, tabulated, and made part of my professional file.
      2. Members of my evaluation committee will be requested to observe my instruction of one unit in Biology 335, discuss their assessment with me, and summarize it in writing.
   B. Assume major responsibility for the laboratory sections of the general education course taught by Bill Brown. One aspect of this will be the development of a laboratory manual.
      1. The manual will be evaluated by the other members of the department and the senior majors.
      2. Design a student evaluation form for laboratory sections and administer it each term. Results will be handled as in II. A. 1. (above).
   C. Continue and complete research project currently in progress.
      1. Upon completion present the research at one of our regular Biology Seminars with the faculty in our consortium colleges.
      2. Write up the research and submit it for publication.
   D. Represent the Division of Natural Science and Mathematics on the Library Committee and chair the Committee on Premedical Education.
      1. Update the brochure on "Premedical Education."
      2. Serve as advisor to all pre-med students. (This will be assessed in our Senior Department Evaluation interviews.)

Exhibit 13. (continued)

3. Arrange for visits of juniors and seniors to two medical schools.
4. Request the chair of the Library Committee to write a brief summary of how I functioned on that committee.

III. Plans for growth and means of evaluation
  A. Videotape three lectures and analyze for self-assessment. Also ask Bill Brown to view and critique them.
  B. In 1979–80 teach one unit in Brown's large general education course. Tape the lectures for personal assessment and use regular evaluation forms for student assessment.
  C. Submit at least two articles for publication (one on my dissertation material and one on the current research project)—copies for file.
  D. In 1980 submit one research grant proposal for funding—copy for file.
  E. Request Sam Williams to work with me on improving my examination techniques. I will ask him to critique previously used examinations and assist me in formulating new ones. In some of my smaller classes I will experiment with oral rather than written exams. Any improvement in this area should be obvious to Sam and should show up on the student evaluation forms.
  F. Obtain a research appointment in industry for the summer of 1980. Report on this experience in my self-assessment statement and request immediate supervisor to submit a letter of evaluation.
  G. Eat in the student dining hall more frequently and occasionally invite students over to our home. Report in self-assessment statement.

IV. Resources needed

A. Research Project		$425
Student assistant	$350	
Typing/Publication costs	75	
B. Printing		600
Laboratory manual	250	
Premedical brochures	350	
C. Travel		325
Professional meeting	175	
Visit medical schools	150	
Total Budget		$1,350

V. Evaluation committee
Bill Brown, Sam Williams, and John Jones (student) have agreed to serve as my evaluation committee and prepare a summary evaluation of my performance. I intend to meet with them every six months or so to assess my progress. In addition to the evaluation means cited above, at the end of the contract period I will write my own comprehensive self-assessment statement.

instructor integrate the course with others that preceded it or that will follow it?

2. *Textbooks, handouts, reading and reference lists, syllabi:* Are they current and relevant? Are they at an appropriate level of difficulty and challenge for the class? Do they fit in with the course outline and supplement lectures and class discussions?

3. *Lecture notes:* Are they well organized and in a logical sequence? Are they up-to-date? Do they include useful examples and varying viewpoints?

4. *Assignments and projects:* How do they fit into course objectives? Are they relevant learning experiences or "busy" work? Are assignments and projects coordinated with the rest of the syllabus material? Are sample problems and lab reports adequately presented to broaden the students? How good is the quality of student projects and reports?

5. *Examinations and grading:* Do exams assess a wide range of skills and knowledge (see Chapter Five)? Are they used as teaching devices (for example, are wrong answers explained)? How are grades assigned—what standards are used? How do exams relate to course objectives? Is there evidence that most students have attained desired objectives?

Although self-evaluations are of limited use for administrative purposes, they can help with instructional improvement. Discrepancies between self-ratings and other sources such as student ratings serve as catalysts for change. Video and audio playbacks help in the self-analysis of teaching. Self-assessment, student ratings, and videotaping are used together in the Clinic to Improve University Teaching at the University of Massachusetts (see Berquist and Phillips, 1977, for a full description of the process).

The individual stress that frequently accompanies self-confrontation may explain the limited use of videotaping on the many campuses where it is available. Individual development plans and growth contracting involve all faculty members, whether tenured or not and whether good or poor as teachers, and thus do not identify and isolate only the weakest teachers for remediation, nor do they depend on voluntary participation. By integrating analysis and remediation, growth contracting contributes to evaluation for tenure and promotion as well as for instructional improvement. Colleges that adopt it, however, need to provide at least some of the financial support required to support it, along with personal assistance to the faculty members involved.

FOUR

Evaluations
by Colleagues

At most colleges and universities, colleagues are a major source of information in evaluating faculty performance for promotion purposes. Peers provide a perspective that differs from that of supervisors or students, a perspective that is particularly important when those colleagues within a department and from other institutions are asked to independently assess a faculty member's scholarship and research productivity. Colleagues are also used extensively in assessing teaching and other faculty activities. A variety of procedures is used to choose those who make the assessments and the factors to be assessed.

When used for tenure or promotion decisions, colleague assessments may be distorted by mutual backscratching or by professional jealousy. One study found that colleague ratings were related to office location (Wood, n.d.). In some systems, each member evaluates every other member—similar to the practice in some military training programs. This approach endangers morale. One institution, experimenting with a system that included both colleague and student ratings of teachers, found a strong faculty reaction against the use of colleague ratings for administrative purposes but a willingness to accept student ratings (Fenker, 1975). Eventually colleague evaluation was sacrificed so that the less objectionable student instructional rating form could be implemented campuswide.

Colleague evaluation of teaching is a sensitive and questionable area, as indicated by research evidence.

What Does Research Report About Colleague Ratings of Teaching?

Most studies of colleague evaluations of teaching effectiveness involve a single, overall rating based on whatever information is available. These ratings (or rankings) are then compared with ratings of the same group of teachers made by students or administrators.

In these studies, faculty members did not visit each others' classes systematically, if at all. On what basis, then, did they judge their colleagues' ability? It is possible that classroom performance can be inferred from the way a teacher acts in department meetings and informal discussions, or that faculty members rely on what they hear from students. The wide use of formal student ratings may contribute to this common knowledge, especially when ratings are made public. Indeed, the researcher in one study acknowledged that the high correlation between peer and student ratings may have been due to a general knowledge of student ratings many teachers had received (Murray, 1972).

Blackburn and Clark (1975) collected ratings for forty-five faculty members in a small liberal arts college in the midwest. Each faculty member rated every other teacher in that curricular division, with a median number of four colleague ratings per teacher. Administrator ratings of each teacher—by the president, academic deans, and department heads—were also collected. Ratings by colleagues and administrators were fairly similar, as were ratings by colleagues and students (both sets of correlations were in the low .60s). Maslow and Zimmerman (1956) report a correlation of .69 between colleague and student ratings of faculty members in their own department. The highest correlation was reported by Murray (1972): .87 for thirty-two teachers rated by their students and eight of their colleagues. Similar studies with elementary and secondary school teachers produced the same kind of results (Morsh and Wilder, 1954). Correlations of this magnitude indicate substantial but incomplete agreement among the various rating groups.

One might therefore ask how colleague ratings based on classroom observation rather than on teaching reputation compare to student ratings. How reliable would these evaluations be? Investigating these questions by analysis of colleague and student ratings at an institution in its first year of operation, Centra (1975) reasoned that colleagues would use classroom observation as the basis for their appraisal since teaching reputations were not yet established. Evidence from this study indicates that such ratings based *primarily* on classroom observation would not be sufficiently reliable to use in making tenure, promotion, and salary decisions—or would require investing more time in visitations or in training sessions.

Items selected for colleague ratings were those that could be observed during a class visit—whether instructors used class time well, whether they raised challenging questions or problems for discussion, to what extent they used examples or illustrations for clarification. Some global items were also included: the overall effectiveness of the instructor, the quality of the lecture, the class discussions, and the textbook(s). Teachers were visited by colleagues from their own and other departments and colleges, and each teacher was observed and rated twice by each of the three colleagues, a total of six separate ratings.

The first finding was that colleagues were generous in their ratings. On the item evaluating overall instructor effectiveness, 94 percent were either "excellent" or "good"; student ratings for the same instructors were also favorable, but not to the same extent as colleagues' ratings. A second finding showed colleague ratings to be not statistically reliable; the average correlation among ratings by different colleagues was about .26 for each item. This low reliability casts doubt on the value of colleague ratings as they were collected in this study. If more colleagues visited each teacher, however, the average of their responses could be more reliable, just as test scores can increase in reliability when the number of test items is increased. Several visits to each class by at least a dozen colleagues, however, would be a time investment that many faculty members would be unwilling or unable to make. Another possibility is to "train" faculty members in what to observe as evidence of good teaching, since trained observers make sounder judgments than untrained observers. Colleague appraisal of teaching practices might be made more reliable in this manner, assuming a consensus were reached on some general principles of effective teaching.

Students and colleagues were in reasonable agreement in rating such specific classroom behaviors as the extent to which the instructor used examples or illustrations to clarify the material, but for most items there was little agreement. This can be attributed in part to the limited amount of time colleagues spent observing instruction as well as the limited number of observers. In judging the instructor's overall effectiveness, for example, not only was there inadequate agreement between student and colleague groups but, as noted earlier, colleagues did not agree among themselves.

What Role Should Colleagues Play in Faculty Evaluation?

Colleagues can properly and systematically appraise other faculty on a wide range of dimensions without necessarily visiting each other's classes. The use of colleague evaluation questionnaires and rating techniques is one way that this can be done.

Colleague Evaluation Questionnaires. Items to be used in a faculty questionnaire were suggested in a study by Hildebrand, Wilson, and Dienst (1971). Starting with sixty-seven items that described the behavior of the best teachers as identified by 119 faculty members, the pool was eventually pared to twenty-eight items to which the majority of faculty members could respond without necessarily attending their colleagues' lectures or seminars. The selected items were grouped through factor analysis into five general areas: "research activity and recognition," "intellectual breadth," "participation in the academic community," "relations with students," and "concern for teaching."

"Relations with students" includes judgments about such questions as whether an instructor "meets with students out of regular office hours" or "recognizes and greets students out of class," behavioral aspects of questionable merit since most faculty members would know less about a colleague's relations with students than would students themselves. Student responses in this area would be more valid, while colleagues should know more about a faculty member's public service and professional activities not identified in the study. The focus of these researchers on the activities of *effective teachers* may account for this exclusion.

One university produced a colleague evaluation form by modifying the first three dimensions from the Hildebrand-Wilson-Dienst study and adding public service and associated professional activities. The thirty-item questionnaire is reproduced in Exhibit 14. As noted in the directions, colleagues were told to base their ratings on a comparison between a particular individual and other members of the department or division. Responses to a form such as this often do not result in much differentiation between members of a department in spite of the specific directions; some departments have therefore employed a forced-choice or ranking system. In one twelve-person department, for example, members were asked to select the four peers whom they would rate highest in teaching, research, and service (Swanson and Sisson, 1971). Selections were made by considering all three dimensions together, with current faculty vitas used as a partial basis for the decision. After collecting ratings for two successive terms, faculty members were rank-ordered according to the number of times each was nominated; wherever large differences in the mean ranks occurred—Swanson and Sisson called these "natural breaks"— teachers were put into separate categories. This resulted in two members being placed in the A category, four in B, three in C, two in D, and one in the F category. These general colleague ratings were then given the same weight as student and chairman ratings and were used by a committee in making salary, tenure, and promotion recommendations.

Such evaluation questionnaires or ranking systems are used by very few departments, perhaps because little is known about the reliability of ratings collected in this manner or about their validity. Formal colleague questionnaires can be extremely divisive. The work of a department or institution benefits from cooperation in teaching as well as in research and curriculum development. A formal evalua-

Exhibit 14. Faculty Colleague Evaluation Questionnaire

Individual Evaluated: _____ Department _____

On the average I have contact with him: Daily _____ Weekly _____

Monthly _____ Bimonthly _____ Occasionally _____

Listed below are a number of statements which describe aspects of faculty behavior. Rate your colleague on each of these items by marking the appropriate response category. Your ratings should be based on a comparison between the particular individual and the other members of his department/division. If you feel that you cannot rate him on a particular item or that the item is not applicable for his work, then mark the response category labeled "undecided."

Code
L   =Low Score
BA =Below Average Score
A   =Average Score
AA =Above Average Score
H   =High Score
U   =Undecided, Not Applicable

Evaluate your colleague in terms of the degree to which he:

Scale 1.   Research Activity and Recognition

1. Has gained national or international recognition for his work   L   BA   A   AA   H   U
2. Has done work with which you are familiar   L   BA   A   AA   H   U
3. Does original and creative work   L   BA   A   AA   H   U
4. Expresses interest in the research of his colleagues   L   BA   A   AA   H   U
5. Is actively engaged in research work or professional activities (not related to teaching)   L   BA   A   AA   H   U
6. Keeps current with developments in his field L   BA   A   AA   H   U
7. Has done work to which you refer in teaching   L   BA   A   AA   H   U
8. Does quality work   L   BA   A   AA   H   U

Scale 2.   Intellectual Breadth

9. Seems well read beyond the subject he teaches   L   BA   A   AA   H   U
10. Is sought by you or others for advice on research   L   BA   A   AA   H   U
11. Is sought by you or others for advice on academic matters   L   BA   A   AA   H   U

Exhibit 14. (continued)

12. Can suggest reading in any area of his
    general field   L   BA   A   AA   H   U

Scale 3.   Participation in the Academic Community

13. Attends many lectures and other events
    on campus   L   BA   A   AA   H   U
14. Is involved in faculty organizations or
    committees   L   BA   A   AA   H   U
15. Is involved in campus activities that are
    associated with students   L   BA   A   AA   H   U
16. Is an active participant in the affairs of
    the academic community   L   BA   A   AA   H   U
17. Is someone with whom you have discussed
    your teaching   L   BA   A   AA   H   U
18. Expresses interest and concern about the
    quality of his teaching   L   BA   A   AA   H   U
19. Expresses interest or concern for the
    problems of students   L   BA   A   AA   H   U
20. Is available and willing to talk with
    students on matters of concern   L   BA   A   AA   H   U

Scale 4.   Associated Professional Activities

21. Discharges intra-university duties in an
    effective manner   L   BA   A   AA   H   U
22. Meets deadlines   L   BA   A   AA   H   U
23. Cooperates with others   L   BA   A   AA   H   U
24. Works well as a member of a committee   L   BA   A   AA   H   U
25. Follows through on committee work by
    appropriate actions and communications   L   BA   A   AA   H   U
26. Makes a positive contribution to the
    progress of his academic unit through
    committee participation   L   BA   A   AA   H   U

Scale 5.   Public Service or Consulting

27. Makes his talent and time available to the
    external community   L   BA   A   AA   H   U
28. Is recognized as an active citizen by the
    community   L   BA   A   AA   H   U
29. Serves his profession and community by
    service consistent with his primary
    obligation as a teacher-scholar   L   BA   A   AA   H   U
30. Is asked to serve as a consultant to other
    organizations   L   BA   A   AA   H   U

tion system in which each member appraises—and is, in turn, appraised by—all others will undermine the needed cooperation and collegiality.

Other Rating Procedures. Within a department, colleague evaluation of candidates for tenure or promotion is more commonly handled by written assessment signed by senior faculty or by the chairman. A few departments use an "anonymous group" approach in which colleagues are nominated and selected to evaluate candidates being considered for promotion or tenure. French-Lazovik (n.d.) describes the procedure at one university. The faculty candidate nominates five colleagues from his own or a related department to serve as evaluators. Three of these five nominees are chosen by the dean, who adds three more to the list, making sure that no rater is competing for rank or salary with the person under evaluation (thus, only tenured people serve) and that at least two members of the committee are from outside the candidate's department but in a related field. These six members (the number can vary if necessary) form a secret committee that never meets, nor are the six aware of the identity of the other members. They also do not know who nominated them and are advised to keep their appointment confidential. Committee members judge performance independently after studying each candidate's dossier, and the six written statements are then pooled by the dean for each characteristic judged—knowledge of the field, professional recognition, teaching effectiveness, and other pertinent factors. These pooled judgments correlate well with evaluations provided by different groups of colleagues (Guthrie, 1954). Average ratings of colleague groups also tend to be stable from one year to the next (Wood, n.d.).

The procedure described by French-Lazovik—which she attributes to Edwin Guthrie, one-time dean at the University of Washington—has several important features. First, both the candidate and the dean (or whoever is collecting the ratings) has some choice in evaluators, yet the candidate is not sure who is definitely on the committee, thus cutting down on contamination by the "friendship" factors noted in peer ratings in other settings (Hollander, 1956). Second, a secret committee that does not meet makes it difficult for one rater to influence others. Finally, committee members from outside the department can balance occasional bias by members within the department.

A variation of this procedure has both the candidate and the dean select members from a large elected faculty committee on promotions. Anonymity and independence of judgment can be achieved by following the procedures outlined above or variations of them. These advantages may well outweigh evaluations reached in group meetings that allow for exchange of information between committee members. As French-Lazovik argues (p. 6), evaluations made following discussions can be unduly influenced by the more forceful members. "A covert advocacy or oppositional stance on the part of a peer can often be couched in what appears to be an unbiased and reasoned argument. Even seemingly objective committee discussions are not free of personality interactions based on friendship, charisma, or respect for another's status; nor do they prevent the interplay of factors such as a desire to please, a history of exchanged favors, or an unwillingness to speak up in the presence of stronger individuals who thereby wield disproportionate influence."

The major drawback to the anonymous group procedure is that ratings for different faculty members are more difficult to compare because they are based on different raters. Some colleagues will be more lenient than others, so judgments could boil down to the "luck of the draw." Should there be little agreement among the judges, another set of colleagues should be selected.

Departments within a single university can adopt a variety of procedures in colleague evaluation. The sixty departments at Kansas State University, for example, use several options (Hoyt, 1977). There is wide divergence on such basic issues as what is rated, how it is rated, and who does the rating. Some collect ratings on such specific characteristics as whether the candidate keeps up to date in the discipline, fulfills curriculum responsibilities, and the like; others prefer to collect overall ratings of effectiveness through general written comments or with a numerical scale; one department asked members to rank the three most effective teachers. Some collect ratings from all department members; others use only tenured faculty; a few select colleague evaluators at random. One large department of eighty people, for example, assembles an anonymous group of raters by asking each faculty member to identify others whom he or she could rate on teaching, on research, or on service; it uses the computer to select at random a group of five colleagues who presumably can rate a particular individual on each of the three functions (fifteen colleagues in all). Group members then complete a numerical rating form for whatever faculty function they are asked to judge. Ratings are averaged for teaching, research, and service for each faculty member. This procedure is most appropriate in large departments and provides a means of selecting a committee of judges among presumably qualified raters. It differs from the model described by French-Lazovik in that the raters rather than the ratees help to determine the committee. It is fairly time consuming, however, and faculty members may regard it as intrusive and counterproductive.

What Role Should Colleagues Play
in Evaluation for Tenure and Promotion?

In developing a system of colleague evaluation for personnel decisions, determination must be made on what is evaluated, who will evaluate, and how they will proceed.

What Is Evaluated? How much emphasis is put on teaching, research, and service performance in tenure and promotion decisions not only varies among departments, particularly in multipurpose institutions, but depends on the different responsibilities held by individuals within departments. Each department needs to work out its own specific procedures and standards in what will be assessed and how colleagues are to be used. Faculty members should, of course, know in advance what is expected of them and how they will be evaluated. They should also have the opportunity to help develop the colleague evaluation system since their acceptance is necessary if it is to work at all.

There is no question about colleague judgment on research and scholarship quality. Their opinions regarding a peer's publications and research can shed light on the quality of research and scholarship to supplement the usual quantity dimension. Together with the chairman, colleagues might also assess a faculty member's committee work, including that on M.A. theses and Ph.D. dissertations, and consider how well the candidate cooperates with others in the department on such matters as arranging schedules and examinations. But what about colleague judgments of teaching effectiveness?

For both instructional improvement and administrative decision making, colleagues should be in a position to judge those aspects of teaching that involve the substance rather than the process itself—such things as the choice of text, the course syllabus and objectives, the reading lists and materials used in instruction, and assignments and examinations. They can assess such characteristics as the extent to which a faculty member has mastered the discipline, keeps up to date in the field, and fulfills curriculum responsibilities. They can also examine the basis on which the instructor assigns grades by obtaining a sample of examinations, papers, and projects in the course together with the grades and comments given to students. Grade distribution information (compared to the same information from other courses with students of similar ability) may also indicate whether a teacher has been especially lenient.

Colleagues could assess these aspects of teaching without necessarily setting foot inside the instructor's classroom. If such visits are conducted, they might supplement the above. Research thus far, however, indicates that ratings based primarily on classroom observation would in most instances not be sufficiently reliable to use as a basis for decisions on tenure and promotion—at least, not without faculty members investing considerable time in visitations or training sessions.

Who Should Participate? Rather than having each faculty member rate all others—often a divisive and counterproductive procedure—selections might be made among senior colleagues who are not in competition for the tenure or promotion slots. The size of the department affects the choice of evaluators. Large departments rely on intra-departmental committees; at small institutions, colleagues are chosen from similar departments or a college-wide evaluation committee is formed. Colleagues in other institutions can be called on concerning scholarship, research, and professional participation. This group, however, is in no position to say anything about teaching competence.

A somewhat anonymous internal group of colleagues, selected through procedures described earlier, can provide frank and potentially less biased judgments; if the group never meets as a committee, the judgments are also independent. Group discussions allow information about the candidate to be shared, but decisions made at such meetings can be highly influenced by the stronger members of the group. Members might exercise more independent judgment if they were trained in what to look for in the dossiers and the evaluation information submitted to them, but promotion committees are seldom trained in this regard, especially in assessing evidence in teaching effectiveness. Faculty or instructional development personnel could provide such training. These specialists focus on formative evaluation or teaching improvement activities—and certainly their involvement in tenure and promotion decisions for individual faculty members would be unwise—teachers would be less likely to seek their assistance. But they could work with department or institution-wide promotion committees to establish general criteria of teaching effectiveness.

Finally, regarding procedures for these evaluations, some departments use numerical rating scales or ranking systems, but written comments may provide better information. This is especially true when a small number of judges is involved, as is usually the case with colleague ratings. A series of open-ended questions dealing with the areas mentioned earlier can be useful in eliciting such comments. The written comments could be accompanied by a numerical rating to summarize the information for personnel decisions.

How Can Colleague Evaluations Be Used for Instructional and Course Improvement?

Whether faculty members can help to improve each other's course content and teaching methods depends, no doubt, on who is involved and what procedures are used. Little improvement comes from occasional class observation by colleagues or administrators who do not know what to look for or who may not be particularly effective teachers themselves. One study (Tuckman and Oliver, 1968) found negative results from supervisor comments because, the researchers surmised, the teachers did not think the supervisors had much basis for judgment. On the other hand, observations by skilled, experienced colleagues or teaching/course improvement specialists can be extremely useful. The Centra (1976a) survey of 756 colleges and universities indicates that formal or informal colleague assessments are less effective than consultation with expert faculty or work with master teachers.

A general guide to making more valid appraisals is given in Exhibit 15. Developed by members of the University of Illinois Office of Instructional Resources (Diamond, Sharp, and Ory, 1978), it is

Exhibit 15. Outline of Colleague Observation Guide

A. Content Suitability
   - Relationship to course syllabi, assigned readings
   - Content is worth knowing
   - Content represents current thinking in discipline
   - Presentation of divergent viewpoints
   - Level of difficulty of material

B. Organization of the Content
   - Logical sequence of topics
   - Pace of the lecture, discussion topics
   - Provision of summaries and syntheses
   - Appropriate use of class time

C. Instructor's Clarity of Presentation
   - Definition of new terms, concepts, principles
   - Relevance of examples
   - Relationship to lab and discussion group assignments

D. Instructor's Questioning Ability
   - Asks variety of types of questions (rhetorical, open-ended, short answer)
   - Engages class members in discussion
   - Allows and encourages students to respond to each other
   - Directs discussion that is centered on the intended topic

E. Instructor's Style
   - Stimulates student thinking
   - Engages student in problem solving activities
   - Appropriate modeling behavior
   - Professional and ethical behavior

F. Instructor-Student Interactions
   - Reinforces and encourages student contributions
   - Creates stiff versus relaxed atmosphere
   - Demonstrates mutual respect
   - Personal mannerisms and teaching style (voice, vocabulary) are suitable

Source: Improving Your Lecturing, Diamond, Sharp, and Ory (1978).

useful to faculty members in viewing each other's course materials and class sessions. Colleagues from similar academic disciplines are appropriate judges for most of the areas listed. The authors suggest using specific rating items under each category (see Exhibit 16) for a "colleague videotape review." Instructors ask from one to three colleagues to view a videotape of their class and to comment on it. Rating

**Exhibit 16. Suggested Categories and Items
For Colleague or Self-Review of Videotaped Classes**

Importance and Suitability of Content

Directions: *Respond to each of the statements*   3=Very Satisfied
             below by circling the number which   2=Satisfied
             most closely corresponds to your   1=Needs Improvement
             observation.   NA=Not Applicable

1. The material presented is generally accepted by
   colleagues to be worth knowing.   3   2   1   NA
2. The material presented is important for this group
   of students.   3   2   1   NA
3. Students seem to have the necessary background to
   understand the lecture material.   3   2   1   NA
4. The examples used drew upon students' experiences.   3   2   1   NA
5. When appropriate, a distinction was made between
   factual material and opinions.   3   2   1   NA
6. When appropriate, appropriate authorities were cited
   to support statements.   3   2   1   NA
7. When appropriate, divergent viewpoints were
   presented.   3   2   1   NA
8. A sufficient amount of material was included in the
   lecture.   3   2   1   NA

   Circle one if appropriate:

   a. too much material was included.
   b. not enough material was included.

Other Comments:

Organization of Content

Introductory Portion

1. Stated the purpose of the lecture.   3   2   1   NA
2. Presented a brief overview of the lecture content.   3   2   1   NA
3. Stated a problem to be solved or discussed during
   the lecture.   3   2   1   NA
4. Made explicit the relationship between today's and
   the previous lecture.   3   2   1   NA

Body of Lecture

5. Arranged and discussed the content in a systematic
   and organized fashion that was made explicit to
   the students.   3   2   1   NA
6. Asked questions periodically to determine whether too
   much or too little information was being presented. 3   2   1   NA

Exhibit 16. (continued)

7 .Presented information at an appropriate level of
   "abstractness."   3   2   1   NA
8. Presented examples to clarify very abstract and
   difficult ideas.   3   2   1   NA
9. Explicitly stated the relationships among various ideas
   in the lecture.   3   2   1   NA
10. Periodically summarized the most important ideas
    in the lecture.   3   2   1   NA

Conclusion of Lecture

11. Summarized the main ideas in the lecture.   3   2   1   NA
12. Solved or otherwise dealt with any problems
    deliberately raised during the lecture.   3   2   1   NA
13. Related the day's lecture to upcoming presentations.   3   2   1   NA
14. Restated what students were expected to gain from
    the lecture material.   3   2   1   NA

Other Comments:

Presentation Style

Voice Characteristics

1. Voice could be easily heard.   3   2   1   NA
2. Voice was raised or lowered for variety and emphasis.   3   2   1   NA
3. Speech was neither too formal nor too casual.   3   2   1   NA
4. Speech fillers, for example, "okay now," "ahmm,"
   etc. were not distracting.   3   2   1   NA
5. Rate of speech was neither too fast nor too slow.   3   2   1   NA

Nonverbal Communication

6. Established eye contact with the class as lecture began. 3   2   1   NA
7. Maintained eye contact with the class.   3   2   1   NA
8. Listened carefully to student comments and questions.   3   2   1   NA
9. Wasn't too stiff and formal in appearance.   3   2   1   NA
10. Wasn't too casual in appearance.   3   2   1   NA
11. Facial and body movements did not contradict speech
    or expressed intentions. (for example, waited for
    responses after asking for questions.)   3   2   1   NA

Other Comments:

Clarity of Presentation

1. Stated purpose at the beginning of the lecture.   3   2   1   NA
2. Defined new terms, concepts,and principles.   3   2   1   NA
3. Told the students why certain processes, techniques,
   or formulae were used to solve problems.   3   2   1   NA
4. Used relevant examples to explain major ideas.   3   2   1   NA
5. Used clear and simple examples.   3   2   1   NA

Exhibit 16. (continued)

6. Explicitly related new ideas to already familiar ones.	3	2	1 NA
7. Reiterated definitions of new terms to help students become accustomed to them.	3	2	1 NA
8. Provided occasional summaries and restatements of important ideas.	3	2	1 NA
9. Used alternate explanations when necessary.	3	2	1 NA
10. Slowed the word flow when ideas were complex and difficult.	3	2	1 NA
11. Did not often digress from the main topic.	3	2	1 NA
12. Talked to the class, not to the board or windows.	3	2	1 NA
13. The board work appeared organized and legible.	3	2	1 NA

Other Comments:

Questioning Ability

1. Asked questions to see what the students knew about the lecture topic.	3	2	1 NA
2. Addressed questions to individual students as well as the group at large.	3	2	1 NA
3. Used rhetorical questions to gain students' attention.	3	2	1 NA
4. Paused after all questions to allow students time to think of an answer.	3	2	1 NA
5. Encouraged students to answer difficult questions by providing cues or rephrasing.	3	2	1 NA
6. When necessary, asked students to clarify their questions.	3	2	1 NA
7. Asked probing questions if a student's answer was incomplete or superficial.	3	2	1 NA
8. Repeated answers when necessary so the entire class could hear.	3	2	1 NA
9. Received student questions politely and when possible enthusiastically.	3	2	1 NA
10. Refrained from answering questions when unsure of a correct response.	3	2	1 NA
11. Requested that very difficult, time-consuming questions of limited interest be discussed before or after class or during office hours.	3	2	1 NA

Other Comments:

Establishing and Maintaining Contact with Students

Establishing Contact

1. Greeted students with a bit of small talk.	3	2	1 NA
2. Established eye contact with as many students as possible.	3	2	1 NA
3. Set ground rules for student participation and questioning.	3	2	1 NA

Exhibit 16. (continued)

4. Used questions to gain student attention.	3	2	1	NA
5. Encouraged student questions.	3	2	1	NA

Maintaining Contact

6. Maintained eye contact with as many students as possible.	3	2	1	NA
7. Used rhetorical questions to re-engage student attention.	3	2	1	NA
8. Asked questions which allowed the instructor to gauge student progress.	3	2	1	NA
9. Was able to answer students' questions satisfactorily.	3	2	1	NA
10. Noted and responded to signs of puzzlement, boredom, curiosity, and so on.	3	2	1	NA
11. Varied the pace of the lecture to keep students alert.	3	2	1	NA
12. Spoke at a rate which allowed students time to take notes.	3	2	1	NA

Other Comments:

Source: Diamond, Sharp, and Ory (1978).

specific aspects of the taped lecture is suggested, but commenting informally would make the procedure less threatening and the feedback more useful. Members of the Office of Instructional Resources also suggest that peers be given a mini-lesson, ten to twenty minutes in length; this allows the teacher to try out new ideas or approaches and to get their colleagues' reactions. Presumably, it also exposes members of the peer group to different concepts. (Exhibit 16 is also suitable for class observations.)

On the premise that teachers learn a great deal about their own teaching by helping others, Sweeney and Grasha (1978) initiated "peer development triads" in which teams of three faculty members work together for one or more terms to help each other assess and improve their instruction, using the following procedure:

1. *Goal setting.* Team members specify in writing two or three major instructional goals each has for the class session to be observed.
2. *First meeting of teams.* Members share and help clarify each other's goals. Each member also lists the types of behavior on

which others should focus—organization of the presentation, questioning procedures, or the way a lab experiment is handled. What observational techniques will be used is determined at this first meeting: some may rely on videotapes, others may collect student reactions, and others may design their own visitation questionnaires.

3. *Classroom observation.* The instructor tells the class that two visitors will be present as observers. Students are given the reason for the visits and alerted to the possibility that the visitors may question them after class.

4. *Team meets for discussion.* Within a week of each visit, observers reconstruct details of the sessions, indicating the positive and the negative aspects in that order. These comments should focus on types of behaviors identified in step 2. After discussion, the instructor selects two or three things to work on before the next observation period.

5. *Next steps.* The teams determine how well they work together and what changes may be needed. The cycle beginning with step 1 is repeated for additional sets of observations.

Among the forty teams that volunteered to use this approach, Grasha (1977) found that one in four consisted of faculty members from the same discipline. The team needs six to eight hours of training by a teaching development specialist; without this, members often did not know how to guide their classroom observations or used improper consulting methods with colleagues (such as telling them how to teach).

Training different triads of faculty members is, therefore, a necessary part of the peer development team approach. It is also somewhat time consuming for both the faculty members and the trainer. An alternative is to train one small group of colleagues as consultants in assessment and improvement teachniques; an example is the "Peer Teaching Assessment" service at the University of Bridgeport. Adapted from the University of Massachusetts' Clinic to Improve University Teaching model (Berquist and Phillips, 1977), the service features a team of four trained faculty members from different disciplines. It is understood that the information they gather will be kept in strict confidence. One consultant observes and videotapes a few of the teacher's classes and collects and analyzes student ratings and reactions in order to get a picture of the instructor's teaching style and interaction with students. The team consultant discusses these impressions with the teacher. The two may agree on changes in teaching style or on the adaptation or refinement of a new technique, and the consultant helps in making these alterations. At the end of the semester, another set of observations and assessments is collected to determine the effectiveness of the approach.

Each of these procedures relies heavily on classroom observations and, even though such information is not intended for administrative purposes, some faculty members are reluctant to invite others into their classrooms. As mentioned, colleagues can make judgments and suggestions without observing classes. An approach described by Hoyt and Howard (1978) is to have a group of eight faculty members meet for a semester to explore teaching issues, to consider each other's classroom teaching, and to discuss teaching methods. Howard found this to be helpful, as indicated by changes on student ratings. Departments have also improved both the content and the instructional techniques employed by holding information meetings in which members take turns discussing the content of their courses or their plans for dealing with a particular unit. Involving the entire department also ensures that all teachers, good and bad, are involved in improvement efforts.

Because volunteer services often appeal to good teachers who want to improve rather than to those needing help (Centra, 1976a; Gaff, 1975), a few colleges have begun programs to assess tenured staff members. Earlham College's program is a good example. It involves colleagues in assessing each tenured faculty member every five years until the age of sixty. The focus of the assessment is on improvement during the ensuing five years and no evidence gathered can be introduced in any proceeding to remove tenure. In fact, the college has assured faculty members that the assessment does not imply any lessening of their adherence to the Statement of Principles of the American Association of University Professors (AAUP). The procedure follows ("Assessment and Development. . . ;" 1975, pp. 1–2):

 1. Early in the year, the faculty member being assessed and the academic dean determine which colleague will serve

on a committee of three. This committee will make a final reading and evaluation of the faculty member's dossier. The dean and faculty member identify colleagues and students from whom letters will be requested.

2. A dossier is collected containing: (a) A self-evaluation stressing not only past accomplishments or weaknesses but also the faculty member's professional plans and needs for the next five years; (b) A student evaluation using the standard college form or an alternative if the faculty member thinks it would be more appropriate; (c) Letters from present and past students, and colleagues inside and outside the department; (d) Any additional documentation considered relevant such as syllabi, publications, and the like.

3. During the fall term, the committee works with the faculty member being assessed in preparing the self-evaluation and five-year plan. Class visitations might also be arranged if mutually agreeable. Early in the second term the committee prepares a written report based on their consultations with the faculty member; the report is sent to the dean.

4. After reading the committee's report and the dossier, the dean meets with the faculty member to discuss plans and goals for the next five years and how the College can be of assistance. A half-time consultant on teaching and other faculty members are also available to work with faculty to improve teaching.

The Earlham program to assess tenured faculty involves colleagues at an early stage in reviewing performance and in making suggestions and later in providing assistance. Since tenured staff members should have a periodic assessment and colleagues should take part in the procedure, programs like Earlham's would be excellent models.

FIVE

Measures
of Student Learning

John L. D. Clark

Student achievement under the tutelage of a given instructor is the fundamental indicator of teacher performance in the minds of students and lay observers of the educational scene. The formal evaluation of college instructors for promotion, salary increase, and tenure involves a number of additional considerations, but classroom teaching performance is—according to the self-report of the administrators involved—a major factor (Centra, 1977a; see Chapter One).

Teacher evaluation through student achievement testing seems to be straightforward, but in close examination of its theoretical and practical implications several problems appear which must be resolved before it can be used in instructional assessment.

John L. D. Clark is a senior examiner in the higher education and career programs at the Educational Testing Service.

First, the institution or department should specify what is expected of a student as a result of following a particular course. Unless teachers, administrators, and the students themselves understand in detail the intended purpose of the instruction, there is no mutually acceptable yardstick to measure student achievement or teacher effectiveness.

Second, once the goals have been identified, test instruments or other measurement procedures must be developed to measure student accomplishment. Externally published instruments which properly cover the learning goals can be used in a few instances, but in most cases the individual instructor, academic department, or another group should develop such achievement measures.

Third, the test instruments must be administered under optimum conditions for the students. Uncomfortable or noisy testing conditions, excessively lengthy tests, and other administration-related variables can seriously affect student performance in a given testing situation, thus invalidating the results. Test scoring should consider interscorer and intrascorer variation in evaluating non–multiple-choice (essay, short-answer) test questions. Such variations can compromise the validity of the student data obtained.

Fourth, testing results must be utilized in ways that are both psychometrically valid and of genuine benefit to the students and instructors involved. On an institutional basis, administrative personnel concerned with faculty development and evaluation should use care in their interpretations. They need to eliminate or adjust for the influence of factors which can affect student testing results independently of "teacher effectiveness" per se—such as the students' prior knowledge of the subject matter, difference in general intelligence or in aptitude for the particular type of learning involved, variation in motivational levels, and similar influences. These variables, rather than true differences in instructional quality, can account for observed increases or decreases over time in student test scores for a given instructor or for score differences among instructors teaching different sections of a given course.

Fifth and finally, the entire student achievement testing program must be supported by both instructors and administrators and be one to which they are willing to give their best professional efforts. Crucial in this regard is the instructor's perception of the uses to which the testing information will be put. Instructors who suspect that student testing results will be used inappropriately— in connection with salary increase, promotion, or other employment-related decisions—will avoid innovative and challenging curriculum development/instruction/measurement activities in favor of more easily taught subject matter on which their students would "show up well," regardless of its ultimate educational value. If, however, they are assured that administrative use of testing data will be restricted to general analyses and that the primary intent of the program is to help the students in their academic development and the instructors in improving their teaching efforts, faculty members will feel much more responsible in planning an effective testing program.

In the following pages, each of the areas outlined above— initial specification of instructional outcomes, development of measurement procedures, and test administration and scoring—is discussed at greater length. Additional references are given to texts or other sources which may be consulted for further discussion. A fourth section considers the use of achievement testing results for feedback to students, instructors, and the institution, emphasizing cautions to be observed in relating student achievement information to the measurement of teacher effectiveness.

A final section contains recommendations for developing and implementing an achievement testing program primarily focused on student accomplishment and course improvement that can reasonably be used in measuring teacher effectiveness, given close adherence to the recommended procedural steps and cautions in interpretation.

How Should Instructional Outcomes Be Initially Specified?

Instructional objectives are crucial to the planning, instruction, and analysis of a comprehensive teaching program. It is thus unfortunate that they are often viewed with suspicion and even hostility by faculty members engaged in course planning or other kinds of instructional development. The need to state instructional objectives in behavioral terms—specifically, that some kind of observable activity on the student's part shows learning success—is a source of confusion and potential resistance. College or graduate level instructors may feel—perhaps heatedly so—that the high level of conceptualization, integration, and sophistication in expression required of their students cannot be "reduced to behavioral objectives," which they associate with elementary and/or rote learning activities.

It is obvious, however, that any student skill or knowledge, regardless of complexity or degree of sophistication, cannot be manifest to the outside world except through observable behavior. This is apparent in skills testing (keypunching, sight-reading at the piano, proper mounting and staining of microscope slides) but less so with respect to mental capabilities or knowledge (naming the bones in the human body, knowing the economic factors that led to the outbreak of the Civil War, analyzing the interrelationships of theme and narrative style in a novel). Short of probing the student's mind with electrodes or using other physical means, however, there is no alternative to asking the student to "behave" by talking, calibrating, writing, and other actions that allow the instructor or observer to infer that the student has indeed acquired the skills or knowledge at issue.

The important question is not whether to teach and test for "behavioral objectives," for there is indeed no alternative. Rather, the question is whether the instructor should think through and describe, in useful detail and as a precondition to both teaching and test preparation, particular student behaviors that will indicate student competence. Without this approach, course objectives become by default whatever student behaviors happen to show up in the final examination or other testing materials used. "Course objectives" of this type—quite possibly springing full-blown from the back of an envelope on the way to class during examination week—are no less behavioral than those that could have been developed in initial course planning but are much less valuable as indexes of student accomplishment and as sources of useful feedback information to the instructor.

In detailing instructional objectives, a useful preliminary step is to develop a series of goal statements covering each major aspect of the course at a somewhat higher level of generality than is appropriate for the instructional objectives themselves. These statements tell both students and colleague faculty the general orientation of the course and constitute the major rubrics under which more detailed objectives can be prepared, as shown in the following examples: (1) introductory accounting course: carry out basic accounting procedures involved in the preparation of balance sheets, income and expense statements, general journals, and general ledgers; (2) French language course: read with a high level of comprehension and reasonable speed typical newspaper and magazine articles from genuine and unedited French sources; (3) political science course: describe in detail the basic characteristics (and major philosophical differences) of capitalistic, communistic, and socialistic economic structures; (4) basic computer course: plan, flowchart, write, keypunch, and run a FORTRAN-based computer program to handle simple statistical or clerical operations. The statement of a single goal is insufficient to cover the desired learning outcomes of a given course. A full description of the elementary computer course, for example, might also include separate goal statements on student knowledge of the binary system and its representation in core storage as well as rudiments of computer console operation.

Goal statements that include each instructional outcome of the course probably will imply the use of measurement techniques other than those limited to paper-and-pencil procedures or similar single testing methods. Although good measurement strategy uses the most straightforward testing technique possible, many outcomes relevant to a particular course require observing student performance, monitoring laboratory exercises, and otherwise obtaining actual work samples of the behaviors in question. To develop and use such procedures may be difficult, but to take the opposite approach—to restrict course goals to aspects which can be most easily tested—is to let the measurement tail wag the instructional dog, to the detriment of student learning and instructional integrity.

After developing the general goal statements, the instructor or faculty group is in a position to design specific instructional objectives that will serve as detailed teaching guides and as patterns for testing procedures. To translate behavioral objectives into testing activities is very simple, since the major conceptual work has already been accomplished. Measurement literature includes manuals on the preparation of instructional objectives and theoretical discussions of the issues involved (Mager, 1962, 1973; Lindvall, 1964; Gronlund, 1970; Bloom, Hastings, and Madaus, 1971). An example of developing one objective and the related testing arrangement for measuring its attainment will demonstrate the general procedure.

In assessing premedical students' knowledge of the bones of the human body, a properly written behavioral objective would describe the student's actions—"pointing to," "matching," "naming aloud," "writing the names of," "answering multiple-choice questions about," and similar responses. The student might name each of several bones as they are pointed to by the instructor on a life-sized skeleton; another possibility might use a line drawing of a human skeleton, its bones identified by numbered arrows and correspondingly numbered multiple-choice questions from which the student chooses the correct name.

Naming the bones aloud with the use of a three-dimensional model involves a direct demonstration of the student's knowledge but requires an elaborate and time-consuming procedure, especially if many students are to be tested. Identifying the bones in a multiple-choice format lends itself readily to group testing but might be criticized as requiring the student only to identify and not to produce the proper terminology.

Such considerations might finally lead to the following learning objective: "Given a line drawing of a human skeleton with certain bones designated by numbered arrows, the student will write out the correct Latin name of each of the designated bones." The instructional objective thus would reflect a useful real-life behavior on the student's part (accurate recall of proper terms from memory, as required in writing up a physical examination, accident report, and such) while providing a testing format in which such behavior could be elicited. Convenience of testing, however, should not take precedence over valid measurements of student knowledge or ability. In many instances, accurate evaluation of a particular type of achievement, such as speaking ability in another language, requires fairly complicated measurement (active speaking by the student and real-time or tape-recorded evaluation by a human listener) in order to maintain the integrity of the evaluation process.

What Measurement Procedures Are Appropriate?

From a systems model point of view, preparing instructional objectives for a given course and developing assessment procedures for these objectives are separable operations. However, it is easier to prepare the initial objectives if one is familiar with a variety of testing techniques and formats to use in developing the actual test instruments. Those techniques and formats can be broadly classified according to the type of response required of the student.

Selected-response techniques, those in which the student is asked to identify the appropriate response, include multiple-choice tests (with their subcategory of true-false items) as the most widely used, and various types of matching questions (such as asking the student to pair a series of vocabulary words with the appropriate printed definitions). *Constructed-response* tests, which require the student to write a response as opposed to identifying the proper answer from among options provided, can range from the very simple fill-in-the-blanks type of exercise through short-answer questions up to and including the writing of lengthy and detailed compositions or essays on specified topics. *Performance* tests require the use of some skilled behavior which is itself the focus of measurement interest (playing a musical instrument, carrying through a particular laboratory process, and so forth). The instructor may be interested in evaluating the process used by the student in performing the task, the product resulting from the performance, or both, depending on the subject matter and the testing intent.

Each of these basic test-format categories has advantages and drawbacks. Questions used in selected-response tests are easy to administer and to score. True-false, multiple-choice, and—somewhat less readily—matching questions can be formatted for use with machine-scorable answer sheets, permitting large volume testing at relatively little cost or manpower involvement. Initial preparation of selected-response questions, however, requires time, effort, and some degree of developed skill.

A technical consideration in selected-response testing is the possibility that any student will be able to answer a particular question correctly through a lucky guess in the absence of any real knowledge of the material tested. This is not crucial to measurement of whole-class performance or even to that of an individual student across an entire test, since adjustments can be made for the proportion of the total test which the students are presumed to have accidentally answered correctly. If the testing intent is to determine, on an item-by-item diagnostic basis, a student's acquisition of particular elements of test content, the "chance correct" problem then becomes a major difficulty: there is always a fairly high possibility (one in two for true-false questions or one in four for A–D multiple-choice items) that a correct response could be fortuitous rather than based on knowledge.

A second question in the use of selected-response techniques is whether student recognition of the appropriate response can be considered a satisfactory instructional outcome as opposed to the ability to actively produce the response in another testing context. Constructed response or production formats may test the desired behavior in a more valid way.

Constructed-response techniques include a wide range of question formats and offer great flexibility for local test development. At one end of the spectrum lies the well-known fill-in-the-blanks or completion item, offering an efficient means of testing student knowledge of basic terminology, definitions, or other relatively discrete aspects of course content. At a middle level, short-answer questions to which the student responds briefly in writing can reliably tap a wide range of student knowledge and analytic abilities. Essay responses have the potential of measuring the student's ability to organize and present relevant information, to defend a particular point of view in topical areas which admit a variety of approaches, and generally to apply, interpret, synthesize, and evaluate various elements of knowledge acquired in the course. The question of scoring reliability assumes greater prominence at this broader end of the constructed-response spectrum. Several techniques can help to increase the objectivity of scoring of essay or other free response tests, but the scoring reliability for tests of this type is generally somewhat lower than for selected-response tests or for the completion/short-answer type.

The observation of student performance is a fairly routine testing technique in such areas as instrumental music and dramatic production; it can also be used to some degree in such fields as accounting, data processing, laboratory sciences (chemistry, physics, biology, and others), archaeology, and foreign languages. Performance-based tests are more difficult to plan, administer, and evaluate than paper-and-pencil instruments of the selected-response or constructed-response type, but they have the advantage of providing face-valid work samples of particular skilled activities in which the student would engage in real-life practice of the discipline. Students who show a high degree of competence on criterion measures of this type can be viewed by both academic staff and lay observers as having achieved important course goals; such a clear demonstration of learning success is not usually possible using paper-and-pencil tests.

In performance measurement, the test developer needs to establish a natural testing situation that is sufficiently well controlled and standardized to provide comparable testing conditions for all examinees and to permit accurate scoring. In general, this involves using somewhat abbreviated representations of real-life situations. In an instrumental music test, for example, the student might be asked to play specified portions of a number of different works that call for a variety of performance techniques and interpretive styles rather than one or two longer selections in their entirety. This permits wider sampling of the student's areas of proficiency and increases the number of critical performance features that can be assessed within a given testing time.

In the literature, Payne (1968), Stanley and Hopkins (1972), and Scannell and Tracy (1975) detail practical information on the preparation of selected response and constructed-response test questions, including discussion of the relative merits of each type of question, while Boyd and Shimberg (1971), Knapp and Sharon (1975), and Fletcher and Clark (1977) supply guidelines for the development and use of performance tests together with examples of testing procedures in many subject areas.

This general overview of testing formats and techniques indicates the wide range of measurement procedures available to individual instructors or faculty groups involved in developing course-based tests of student achievement. Selection of appropriate testing procedures for a given course depends largely on the specific student behaviors called for in the learning objectives for the course. If a major objective of a foreign language course, for example, is a useful level of speaking proficiency, the testing procedures would necessarily involve active speech on the part of the student, although spoken performance is more difficult to elicit and evaluate than written or multiple-choice responses.

Objectives which involve knowledge or intellectual competencies not associated with a particular skilled performance should use the simplest possible testing procedure consistent with adequate measurement of the intended objective. An essay test format used only to check the student's ability to recall a series of facts about a particular topic wastes testing time, is relatively difficult to score, and is potentially less reliable than a short-answer or fill-in-the-blanks format. This reductionist approach should not, however, go below the level of sophistication required to adequately represent the learning objective. If selective, organized, well-documented responses are implicit in the learning objective itself, then the more extensive constructed-response formats should be employed.

A second step in test development is to ensure that the test as a whole will adequately represent or sample the major learning outcomes of the course. With the possible exception of an achievement test on the first lesson of a beginning course, it would be impossible, within any test of practical length, to cover each learning aspect which the student should have acquired. Test content planning thus involves extracting from a large number of potentially testable elements a subset of items which can represent the wide number of similar elements not formally tested.

The definition of operationally similar elements will, in some instances, be relatively automatic. In mathematics, for example, one or two test exercises in solving a quadratic equation could represent quadratic equations in general; students able to solve correctly the test exercises could be presumed able to solve similar quadratic problems not included in the test. Individual test questions in other subject areas, however, may not be so representative. In a French literature course, for example, the student's answer to a question dealing with nineteenth-century drama may not indicate similar performance for nineteenth-century poetry; this would depend in part on the way in which the course was structured (by "century" or "genre"), the nature and extent of outside reading assignments, and so forth. Informed judgment by the instructor, along with the input of subject-matter colleagues, would be needed in these instances.

In choosing samples and planning test content, it is useful to design a specifications table that shows the prospective content areas to be included and the percentage weight to be given each area within the test as a whole. The table should be reviewed to ensure that student objectives are fully represented through actual test questions/exercises or by strong implication based on student performance on other related questions/exercises that are to be included. If adequate "coverage by implication" is at all questionable, relevant material should be explicitly included in the test.

In addition to the simple content area/percentage-of-test approach to test specification, other more elaborate procedures may be followed. A recommended technique is to set up a two-dimensional matrix with subject matter content along one dimension and the six levels of the well-known Bloom taxonomy of the cognitive domain ("knowledge," "comprehension," "application," "analysis," "synthesis," and "evaluation") along the other dimension (Bloom, 1956). Within each cell of the matrix, a percentage figure is used to indicate the proportion of the total test to be devoted to that content/cognitive level combination.

Research on the Bloom taxonomy (Krathwohl and Payne, 1971; Madus, Woods, and Nuttall, 1973) questions the sequencing and operational independence of the higher-level categories of the taxonomy. For theoretical and practical reasons, the test developer may prefer to modify or combine certain of the Bloom levels in preparing the actual test specification matrix. A total of four categories might be used—"knowledge," "comprehension," "application," and "higher level"—with the latter category including all of the last three categories of the original taxonomy.

Full-scale and modified applications of the Bloom taxonomy for test planning in social studies, art education, mathematics, literature, writing, and foreign languages, and several other subject areas are detailed in Bloom, Hastings, and Madaus (1971). Primary emphasis is on secondary-school curricula, but the discussions and examples can be readily extrapolated to undergraduate- and graduate-level contexts.

Other examples of two-dimensional matrix or "grid" approaches to test content specification are available in Payne (1968), and Stanley and Hopkins (1972). In using the Bloom taxonomy or other test specification procedures, the instructor/test developer should try to produce a test that directly reflects the specific behavioral objectives on which the course—and presumably, the detailed instructional activities—have been based. In this light, the various test specification outlines are useful in suggesting the range of student learning outcomes, over and above factual knowledge, that might be included in planning course objectives.

Finally, the test questions/exercises should be assembled in an appropriate sequence, together with necessary student instructions, and the test reproduced in quantity for administration. If more than one question type is included in the test, it is accepted practice to begin with the simplest type and present the more complex exercises later. Multiple-choice questions, for example, should be placed before fill-in-the-blanks; short-answer before essay/composition. Within any given question type, the content should progress from the easiest to the most difficult so that students will not be taken aback by the early appearance of especially difficult items.

Research literature indicates that question placement may affect student performance less than is generally assumed. Sax and Cromack (1966) find that arrangement of multiple-choice items in easy-to-difficult, difficult-to-easy, or random order had no differential effect on undergraduate student performance on an unspeeded test of seventy numerical ability items. Marso (1970) reports similar results for a 103-item final examination in educational psychology. These two studies notwithstanding, it is still probably advisable on psychological grounds to use an easy-to-difficult item arrangement pattern in instructor-developed tests.

The test assembler often gives insufficient attention to student directions accompanying the test. Such basic information as total testing time, separate timing (if any) for test sections, scoring weights for different sections or questions, and (in multiple-choice tests) whether there will be any penalty for guessing should be given in written form as part of the test materials and also read aloud by the instructor if desired. Additional printed instructions for each separate section of the test should describe the particular kinds of response required by the student. This is particularly important when a change in the student's mental set is required, as when a series of multiple-choice questions requires selecting a single inappropriate ("doesn't-fit-with-the-other-options") choice rather than the usual "best" or "most appropriate" answer.

The physical layout of the test directions and questions should minimize any problems in responding attributable to the format of test materials. In any sort of matching exercise, for example, the item to be matched should be on the same or a facing page so that constant turning of the pages is avoided. For essay questions, it is useful to print the essay topic on a separate and removable page so that the student has easy and constant reference to the specific wording of the topic rather than having to flip back for this purpose.

These and other considerations meriting attention during the test assembly and reproduction process are described in detail in Furst (1958), Gronlund (1968), and Stanley and Hopkins (1972). Instructor adherence to such recommendations will help to ensure that the physical presentation of test questions and instructions will facilitate rather than hinder the student's performance on the substantive material of the test.

How Should Tests Be Administered and Scored?

The conditions under which tests are administered and scored, along with the procedures used, must be designed to ensure the measurement validity of the results. The single major concern in administration is to bring students and test materials together in such a way as to minimize the influence of variables other than actual student competence in the subject matter of the test. These other-than-competence variables can be categorized as *student-related, test-related,* and *environment-related.*

Student-related variables affecting test performance can be either psychological or physiological in nature. The former involves the general mental set with which the student enters the testing situation; recent family or personal problems or other individual concerns can result in a performance which does not indicate the student's actual capabilities. Physiological variables include excessive fatigue and other out-of-sorts conditions. Student-related variables are not usually within the effective control of the instructor. However, such practices as scheduling important examinations so as not to coincide with such campus events as homecoming weekend and permitting deferred or make-up tests for students who have serious and documented personal difficulties can be of value.

Test-related variables with a negative influence include the format, as described in the preceding section, and technical problems such as poor reproduction of the test copy and damaged or missing test pages. Total test length, which should be considered at the test planning and assembly stages, is also important. If the examination calls for lengthy written answers, physical writing fatigue may reduce the quantity or quality of the responses regardless of the student's knowledge of the topics involved.

Environment-related variables refer to physical conditions within the testing room—temperature and humidity, noise level, lighting, adequate desk or table space, and similar conditions. There is some evidence that properly motivated students perform well under less than ideal testing conditions (Ingle and DeAmico, 1969), but it is advisable to make sure for any test—and especially for extensive and "important" examinations—that conditions in the room are comfortable and not distracting to the student.

Test scoring is the process of converting the student's behavior—or the observable by-products of this behavior—into discrete categories or numbers that accurately reflect its quality. This requires a scoring procedure—whether applied to selected-response, constructed-response, or performance testing—that will meet the basic criteria of validity, reliability, and practicality.

Validity of scoring refers to the extent to which the scoring procedure is based upon (and hence, reflects) the particular aspects of student achievement at issue in the test. In multiple-choice or other types of selected-response testing, scoring validity is not independent of the question of an item's general validity. If an item properly covers a particular aspect of student knowledge and proficiency, its scoring (the crediting of a correct student response and noncrediting of an incorrect response) can also automatically be considered valid. For constructed-response and performance-based tests, however, the scoring procedure itself can have varying degrees of validity. For example, in a performance test of exhibition diving, a highly valid scoring procedure would cover timing, body positioning throughout the dive, entry into the water, and so forth. An invalid scoring procedure might include judgments based on or influenced by such peripheral considerations as the style of the swim suit or the attractiveness of the diver. In constructed-response testing, attention to such nonrelevant aspects as quality of student handwriting would also tend to lower scoring validity. The well-documented influence of handwriting quality, spelling, and other mechanical aspects (Chase, 1968; Marshall and Powers, 1969; Briggs, 1970; Soloff, 1973; Markham, 1976) must be considered in scoring essays or other tests involving written responses. The influence of these factors may not be completely eliminated from constructed-response testing, but their effect can be minimized by rigorous attention to the content rather than the appearance and expressive style of the student's answers.

Scoring reliability involves both the extent to which a given student's test performance receives the same score from several different judges (interscorer reliability) and the agreement between the scores given to the same test material by a single judge initially and at a later time (intrascorer reliability). Unreliability, either the interrater or intrarater, is a serious measurement problem in that the scoring of the response is affected by the idiosyncrasies of the particular judge evaluating the performance or the time at which the evaluation is carried out. The following recommendations may help to increase scoring reliability of essay-type tests: (1) Prepare, for each question, an answer key or scoring guide outlining the particular elements of the student response to be evaluated and the weight to be assigned to each element. (2) Identify the papers by code numbers or other means that do not identify the student. (3) Score each essay separately; this involves scoring a particular question for the entire group of tests before going on to the next question, rather than scoring all the questions in a single test at one time. This avoids the so-called halo effect in which the quality of a student's response to one question influences the scorer's appraisal of subsequent questions. For the same reason, scores assigned to earlier questions should be concealed from view during the scoring of later questions. (4) Randomly rearrange all test papers after each scoring pass so that particular papers will not be unfairly advantaged by their position in the scoring sequence. (5) Wherever possible, as when the same examination is administered to several sections of a given course, work with other faculty members to score the test on a group basis. It is useful to have each faculty member specialize in particular test questions and score all those questions, and only those questions, across the test papers for all sections.

How Should Test Results Be Used and Interpreted?

The preceding pages described the major theoretical and technical principles involved in planning, developing, administering, and scoring tests of student achievement so as to represent the student's knowledge/performance in a specific instructional area at a particular time. Information obtained from this testing is valuable to the students themselves (in appraising their success in meeting the learning objectives of the course), to the instructors (interested in the test results for individual students and in the performance profile of the class as a whole as an aid in course analysis), and to department chairmen, academic deans, or other administrators who weigh student achievement as one factor in their evaluation of teacher effectiveness.

To the individual student, a basic element of test-based feedback is the total score on the test. This figure gives limited information, however, since it shows only the student's standing in relation to the number of points in a perfect test performance. Separate scores on each subsection of the test, corresponding to major content/performance areas stressed in the course, are more useful. A score at or near the maximum for a given subsection indicates satisfactory accomplishment of the instrumental objectives represented by that section; subsections for which near-perfect performance was not attained indicate course areas in need of further attention by the student.

At a more highly diagnostic level, the student's performance on each separate test question could be reported, either on a right/wrong basis (for multiple-choice or simple completion questions) or as a proportion of maximum score for more extensive questions (say, three points out of five for a short-answer question). A report on each separate item score, together with total scores for major subsections of the test, would be ideal from the student's standpoint—although admittedly more time-consuming for the instructor.

The classroom instructor can use such test-based information as the individual student data cited above in analyzing particular learning problems, for grading purposes, and for class tabulations. The distribution across a given class of total test scores shows general class achievement and identifies particular students who perform at an appreciably higher or lower level than their colleagues. Particularly useful in course review and revision is a more detailed level of analysis that involves tabulating—across all the students in the class—student responses to each item or subsection of items. When a majority of the students perform successfully on a given item or section, the instructor may take pride in the teaching activities for that aspect of the course. Individual questions or test sections on which the students as a whole score poorly may indicate course areas that require the instructor's attention.

Testing results for individual questions help the instructor to monitor and improve the psychometric quality of the tests that he or she prepares. Student responses to a particular essay question, for example, may indicate that the topic was expressed in an ambiguous or misleading way. Student responses to short-answer or fill-in-the-blank questions may reveal that certain questions could be answered ingeniously—and quite correctly—in an unanticipated manner; in such cases, the scoring guide for that question needs to be revised to include additional correct possibilities or the question rewritten so that only a single answer can be considered correct.

Various computer routines available through most college or university testing offices simplify post-administration analysis of multiple-choice questions. Such item-analysis programs typically provide, for each item processed, an item-difficulty index (the percentage of students in the analysis group who answered the question correctly), an item-test correlation index (r-biserial, r-point biserial, indicating the ratio between the student's score on the entire test and on each particular item), and an option-selection analysis (showing the frequency with which the keyed option and each incorrect option [distracter] were chosen by the examinees). Item-difficulty information identifies for the instructor/test reviewer items that are either inappropriately difficult or too easy for the examinee group. The item-test correlation reveals items that behave differently from others in the test and that may contain previously unsuspected ambiguities or other problems. Option-selection analysis identifies both throwaway options (those seen by the examinee group as so patently incorrect that they are rarely chosen) and distracters that are so conceptually close to being correct that they compete with or even surpass the intended key in the proportion of students selecting the option. Careful reworking of the item is indicated in either case.

Computer-based item analysis is recommended wherever the appropriate facilities are available, but simplified analysis procedures involving only paper-and-pencil mathematics can be used quite effectively (Diederich, 1964).

Student and instructor feedback of test results is a relatively straightforward matter, and—if the test instrument has been properly developed—the results can indicate student achievement at the time of testing. The use of student testing data in connection with instructor evaluation is, however, more complicated since it is necessary to rule out factors that could affect the testing results over and above teacher competence as such.

A possible biasing factor is that of prior-to-course student competence, the possibility that some of the students—through earlier course work, independent study, or other means—will already possess many of the knowledges/skills to be covered in the course. In such cases, a large proportion of observed student achievement on an end-of-course examination might be credited to earlier learning opportunities rather than to the instructional effectiveness of the course itself.

The subject matter and instructional level involved govern the degree of concern required in such cases. Prior knowledge and proficiency may, in some instances, be ruled out entirely, as in a beginning FORTRAN course for students reporting no prior study of this coding system. In other cases, however, there is greater likelihood that students will have significant prior ability in or knowledge of the end-of-course achievement areas being tested. In an intermediate-level drawing class, for example, it could be anticipated that most students would enter the class with some degree of proficiency in the relevant techniques. This being the case, the results of a single end-of-course drawing ability test would reflect both initial student competence and course-acquired proficiency in unknown relative proportions, thus making it impossible to isolate the specific instructional effect of the course itself. Other courses involving either proficiency development over an extended period of time (as in dance, dramatics, instrumental music) or the accumulation of factual knowledge (as in biology, history, and other specializations at the undergraduate or graduate level) are subject to the measurement influence of prior competence.

One means of measuring and adjusting for prior student competence is to test students at the beginning of the course as well as at the end; score differences between the two tests would be considered to represent student gain during the course and to reflect teacher effectiveness more accurately than the simple final achievement test scores. This pre-course and post-course comparison, however, involves a number of practical and psychometric difficulties. The need to prepare additional testing materials—hopefully, equivalent (alternate) forms of the end-of-course test—requires substantial faculty time and cost. The possibility that the scoring procedure and/or the standards used in scoring will differ across the relatively long interval between test administrations is a potential statistical problem (except for multiple-choice tests). If whoever judges the test performance is more severe or more generous in the post-course scoring than in the pre-course scoring, the true growth in student achievement will not be accurately represented.

Another statistical complication concerns the difficulty of establishing a satisfactory and consistent metric for student gain independent of the entry level of the students involved. As an example, consider two different sections of a given course; one instructor draws students who are beginning the course at an elementary level (shown by low pre-course scores on a test emphasizing fundamental principles), while the second instructor has a group already familiar with many of the basic concepts of the course (and therefore able to obtain relatively high pre-course scores). At the end of the course, an alternate form post-course test is administered to both sections; the score differences for the first class are found to be substantially greater than those for the second class.

It is tempting to conclude that the instructor of the first class did a better teaching job than the instructor of the second class, since the score gain of the students in the first class was appreciably greater. This interpretation is probably unjustified, however, since the two groups of students and their instructors were in reality running two different educational races. The first instructor had the relatively easy task of getting his students to understand basic principles which would enable them to increase their post-course scores considerably. The instructor of the second class had to spend just as much effort in perfecting the more advanced students' command of the subject matter without obtaining correspondingly great increases in test scores, because there was relatively little room for improvement on the later test for students who had already scored at a rather high level on the early test.

This situation reflects one of several psychometric complexities in gain-score use and interpretation that make this approach to student achievement measurement (and, by the same token, teacher effectiveness determinations) a much debated and often criticized technique. For readers interested in the statistical aspects of the gain-score question, there is a comprehensive review article by Linn and Slinde (1977) with further references.

Other sources of teacher-independent variation in end-of-course achievement include differences in general intelligence as measured by the standard IQ tests or in specialized aptitude for a given subject area as measured by appropriate prognostic tests such as the Carroll-Sapon *Modern Language Aptitude Test* (Carroll and Sapon, 1959). Intelligence and aptitude are routinely found to correlate highly with academic success in a variety of educational settings. Variation in the degree of motivation with which students approach particular learning tasks is also clearly associated with subject-matter achievement. The effective teacher can indeed influence student motivation to some extent during the course, but the general level of interest developed by the individual student over a number of years of academic study can seldom be changed appreciably by a single instructor on a short-term basis.

To properly relate observed end-of-course student achievement to instructor competence, it is necessary to adjust for (in statistical parlance, "control for") the influence of general intelligence, aptitude, motivation, and other variables. If, due to the luck of the draw, a particular instructor obtains a class in which the students, on average, rank higher in those variables than students in other similar courses, their higher end-of-course achievement scores may (possibly quite erroneously) be credited to a high degree of instructor competence. By the same token, a group of students ranking relatively low with respect to these noninstructor variables may achieve rather mediocre test results even though the quality of instruction was consistently high. Recent studies (Centra and Creech, 1976; Leventhal, Perry, and Abrami, 1977) indicate that student perceptions of instructor experience and reputation substantially affect student course selection as well as student performance, supporting the notion that students do not randomly assign themselves to instructors when choice is available.

A method of controlling for the influence of noninstructor variables is to measure them directly and then to statistically adjust achievement test scores on the basis of those measurements. For example, in addition to the end-of-course achievement tests, students can take a standardized intelligence test (or this information can be taken from existing files). Through such statistical techniques as the analysis of covariance, achievement test scores of individual students are raised or lowered to adjust for differences in intelligence level or for other measured variables. The new weighted achievement scores for different instructors' classes or other groupings can then be directly compared and analyzed.

Although the use of covariance weightings and other statistical adjustments to control for noninstructor variables is a considerable improvement over the simple analysis of raw test data, this approach is not without its own shortcomings. Each student must take one or more additional tests (or prior testing files must be searched for relevant data) and the information analyzed either laboriously by hand or by computer processing with the procedural assistance of a trained measurement specialist.

A second problem in the use of these techniques is determination of the weighting variable(s) to be used. Variables that correlate highly with observed student achievement in other settings may not have equal weight in the particular application being considered. Regardless of the variables finally selected, it is always possible to make the devil's advocate hypothesis that some further noncontrolled variable other than instructor effectiveness is responsible for the observed differences in weighted scores.

The powerful concept of statistical randomization provides a second method to control for the effects of other-than-instructor variables. In comparing different instructors' classes within a given course, such an approach involves assigning each student to a particular instructor on a completely random basis (as by drawing numbered slips from a pile). It is quite possible in any single use of the randomization technique—say, the assignment of students to classes over a single semester—for the obtained groups to vary significantly on one or more of the variables of interest. Systematic use of this approach over a period of several school terms, however, will make it mathematically highly probable that each instructor will have worked with comparable groups of students. Furthermore, these student groups will be comparable not only in those variables known to affect final course achievement, but in any unknown contributing variables which the evaluators do not need to identify in making effective use of the randomization method.

When it is possible to randomly assign students to different sections of a single course, their test scores can indicate teaching effectiveness of the instructors involved, provided that such comparisons cover a relatively long time period and that operational decisions regarding the instructors are not made until testing results over several school terms have been accumulated. Relatively good or poor testing results for one or two semesters cannot indicate high or low teaching competence, since noninstructor variables may have had a disproportionate influence on those particular occasions. With statistical randomization, however, a consistent pattern of superior or inferior student achievement test scores extending over a number of separate school terms indicates that a given instructor is teaching effectively. A number of factors, including class size and the number of cycles of the course over a given time period, governs the length of time over which such an analysis would have to be carried out. Local consultation with the institutional testing office or statistics faculty would help to establish reasonable guidelines in this regard.

It may be possible in a number of instances, as for simultaneously scheduled sections of a large introductory course, to establish statistically random class groupings. However, students are usually free to self-select the course section most suited to their schedule or favored by them for some other reason. This situation violates a basic principle of true statistical randomization in that assignment to classes becomes not a matter of pure mathematical chance but a result of scheduling happenstance, personal preference, or other factors which are both nonrandom and very difficult to isolate and interpret.

In teacher-effectiveness analyses, comparison of achievement test scores for student-selected class groupings—although on less secure statistical grounds than comparisons based on random assignment—can be of some use provided that extensive scrutiny reveals no systematic bias in the selection process. Any systematic course selection bias (for example, disproportionate concentration of athletic students in morning classes to free their afternoon schedules for sports) will substantially affect the direct interpretability of achievement testing results for different class sections. However, if it can be concluded that students are assigning themselves to classes on an essentially random basis, achievement test comparisons can be carried out—although with greater caution than is required with truly random allocation.

Additional Recommendations

The preceding pages have described major considerations involved in planning, developing, and administering tests of student achievement and in using the testing results both for student evaluation and to determine teacher effectiveness. Following are some additional recommendations to be considered in implementing such a program.

1. Plan and develop the testing program and associated test instruments on a group basis. Of all the recommendations listed, this is probably the single most important. It refers to the formal collaborative effort of all relevant members of a given academic department or other curricular grouping to work jointly on the achievement testing program in that particular area, as opposed to the independent development of testing procedures and content by each individual instructor. Collaboration on test content specification can reflect the best thinking of a number of qualified faculty members rather than the possibly idiosyncratic approach of a single instructor. Peer influence and the synergistic effect of group effort may also result in a more ambitious and comprehensive measurement plan than would otherwise be the case. At the test preparation stage, group review and revision of test questions can raise the psychometric quality of the instruments. Collaboration in scoring, using the procedural guidelines outlined above, can help to ensure a higher level of scoring reliability within and across classroom groupings—a *sine qua non* of valid instructor-based comparison of student performance.

2. Bring faculty and administration members into joint discussion as early as possible and provide for continued communication at all stages of the test development and results-utilization process. Where student achievement information is to be used in connection with evaluating instructor effectiveness, it is important for the administrative staff to be frank with the faculty regarding the anticipated use of student testing results for instructor evaluation purposes. The

academic faculty needs both verbal and procedural assurance that the testing data will be used with attention to appropriate interpretative cautions, that test-related information will be only one of several aspects of instructor performance evaluated, and that the evaluations will extend over a sufficiently long period of time to balance the effects of atypical class groupings or other short-term influences not attributable to teaching performance per se. From-the-beginning discussions, free exchange of viewpoints, and continued collaborative liaison between faculty and administrative staff on all aspects of the achievement testing program can provide these assurances.

3. Plan for a long-term commitment to the achievement testing program. In any properly conducted test development and utilization effort, there is a substantial front-end load of faculty and administrative staff time and of other institutional resources. If the newly developed testing program is abandoned or seriously reduced in scope or institutional priority after only a year or so of operation, the intensive commitment during the developmental phase cannot be effectively amortized. More important, an equitable approach to the measurement of teacher effectiveness would require—for reasons already discussed—consideration of testing results across a longer time span than could be provided by one or even two years of program operation.

4. Provide for evolutionary changes in test content and other aspects of the testing program based on developed experience. The maintenance of a testing program across a span of several years is not incompatible with the gradual improvement of the test instruments themselves or of the score reporting, tabulation, and other feedback processes involved in using test results. In-service programs addressed to measurement topics, periodically scheduled discussions of the status of the testing program and needed changes, and a number of other means can and should be used to keep assessment matters in the minds of both faculty and administration and to stimulate continual improvement of the process.

5. Stress a student-behavior approach to test planning and preparation. Faculty groups involved in test development projects will probably use nonbehavioral terminology in their early discussions of desired student achievement, such as "the student will learn to appreciate Shakespeare's use of simile," "demonstrate a command of complex verb forms," "learn the major parts of plant and animal

cells," and so forth. This may be appropriate at the outset, but the group should move as quickly as possible into a discussion of specific behaviors that will indicate student attainment. Once discussion has focused on student behaviors rather than on unobservable and un-measurable mental operations, it becomes an easy task to identify testing techniques that will elicit the desired behaviors in a valid and administratively practical way.

6. Ensure that the testing approach is determined by the student attainment to be measured, not vice versa. Academic faculty and other groups convened for test development purposes share an unfortunate tendency to focus too quickly on test formats and testing procedures after only a cursory exploration of the student attainments to be measured. In many instances, a particular testing technique such as a multiple-choice or essay test will be proposed and accepted almost immediately, with the result that subsequent discussion of student behaviors and related test content is restricted to the measurement possiblities—and drawbacks—of that testing mode. In such instances, barring a fortunate initial selection of testing mode, the need to conform student attainments to the particular exigencies of that mode may do considerable violence to the comprehensive measurement of those student achievements that should be at issue. It should also be reemphasized that paper-and-pencil techniques may not adequately measure many desired student outcomes; in these cases, test planners must develop performance-based measures despite the greater difficulty in their administration and evaluation.

7. Follow appropriate technical procedures and cautions in preparing, administering, and scoring the student achievement tests. This chapter has permitted only an overview of basic considerations and practices in these crucial areas. Additional resources include measurement textbooks and other references, in-service training opportunities using outside consultants or local testing office staff, and the very important hands-on experience and peer review opportunities provided by faculty group involvement in each of these processes.

8. Make maximum use of obtained testing results. Given the investment required to plan and implement a student achievement testing program through the point of test scoring, the greatest possible amount of test-based feedback should be given to students, instructors, and administrative personnel. This involves computer processing of

test results at both the whole-test and individual-question levels and production of the relevant tabulations and summaries—all of which are well within the capabilities of the typical college or university computer installation. To limit the feedback process solely to the reporting of whole-test data would be to ignore vast quantities of information needed by students in monitoring their own learning accomplishments and by the instructors/test developers in course evaluation and test improvement.

SIX

Assessment of Research, Advising, and Public Service

The goals of an institution and the responsibility of a particular faculty member determine the importance given to research, student advising, and public service. This chapter discusses methods of assessing performance in each of these areas.

How Are Research and Scholarship Evaluated?

With fewer faculty members being awarded tenure and promotions, research and scholarship as well as teaching performance are receiving close scrutiny, focusing in particular on the quality and impact of an individual's work. Studies on the measurement of scientific performance or scholarship agree on little other than the fact that no one criterion is sufficient. In-depth studies of scientific productivity in research organizations, for example, have identified such criteria as productivity and originality in written work, visibility, creativity ratings by supervisors, popularity with members of a research team, and recognition for organizational contributions (Edwards and McCarrey, 1973). Criteria such as those identified in the survey questionnaire (Chapter One) and discussed below are more appropriate for college and university faculty.

Colleagues have always evaluated each others' work as referees for journal articles or in informal discussions. Systematic colleague evaluations play an equally critical role in tenure and promotion decisions. They are particularly important, however, in the assessment of research and scholarship.

The quality of research and scholarship is related to the quantity produced, but the two are not necessarily consistent. In a survey of university physicists, Cole and Cole (1967) found a correlation of .72, while Meltzer (1956), Clark (1957), and Schrader (1978) report slightly lower correlations for other disciplines. (Schrader, for example, found a correlation of .60 between a citations count and the number of publications for a sample of psychology Ph.D.s.) Each of those researchers used the number of citations of published work as an indication of quality. Cole and Cole identified the inconsistent groups as "mass producers" (a relatively large number of papers of little consequence) and "perfectionists" (high in quality but low in quantity). Just under a third of their random sample fell into these categories. Their data suggest, furthermore, that quality research is often rewarded in high ranking departments, while the sheer number of publications is more likely to be used in determining promotions in less prestigious departments.

How Can Quality Be Assessed? Since quality may not always be reflected in a publication count, departments should try other ways of assessing the significance of a person's work. Success is often related to continuity in research, as indicated by a number of articles (or, in some instances, a book) dealing with a particular topic or problem. Such continuity does not mean repetition of subject matter or narrowness of interests, but simply that the person has explored related problems within a particular area (Crane, 1965).

Peers within the institution and those outside are undoubtedly best able to judge the continuity element of a colleague's work as one part of overall quality. In evaluating research in specialized areas, scholars at other institutions are probably essential. Survey results (Centra, 1977a) suggest that peers at other institutions are being increasingly called on for their opinions. If done in a confidential manner, these assessments can be more objective than those of colleagues within an institution who, because of friendships or rivalries, may not always be objective. A sufficient number of colleagues should be surveyed to prevent undue weighting of a single unusually high or unusually low assessment. In eliciting judgments from colleagues, a request for a general estimation is less apt to help than asking specific questions—in particular, questions that touch on the significance of the candidate's accumulated efforts. The form letter (Exhibit 17) includes questions sent by one university to colleagues at other institutions.

**Exhibit 17. Example of Form of Letter
for Use in Requesting Evaluation of Candidate**

Dear _____:

The University of _____ is considering the appointment (promotion) of _____ to the rank of _____, a position which carries tenure. On such appointments we seek expert advice from outside our faculty as well as within it. You have been recommended to us as particularly able to evaluate Dr. _____'s qualifications for this position. We would appreciate your candid opinion of his qualifications, and any other information you can provide that will help in making a wise decision. We are especially interested in the following:

1. The candidate's professional competency.
2. The quality and significance of his professional publications.
3. His national reputation and relative standing in his field.
4. If your own institution had a position available in the candidate's area of competence, would he be given favorable consideration for such a position? Would your response to him be negative, lukewarm, generally favorable, or enthusiastic?

You can be certain, of course, that your reply will be kept in the strictest confidence. If you feel that you are unable to comply with this request, we would welcome any suggestions from you as to who can best supply us with this information.

Thank you for your consideration and help in this matter.

Sincerely yours,

[*Note:* Information on the following additional items should be requested for new appointments.]

5. His teaching ability, if known.
6. His general desirability as a faculty member.
7. His personality and ability to work with people.

A more objective approximation of the quality or impact of a person's work is to note the number of times a person's publications have been cited in subsequent literature. Citations usually signify impact; most scientists cite previous work because they think it is important and want to relate their own work to it. But there are problems in the use of citations, as Cole and Cole (1967, p. 380) point out: "(1) Work of the highest significance often becomes common knowledge very quickly and is referred to in papers without being cited. (2) Citations may be critical rather than positive. (3) The various scientific fields differ in size. If we wish to compare the work of scientists in different fields, we must take into account the number of people actively working in these fields. (4) The significance of scientific work is not always recognized by contemporaries."

This may be why department chairmen and academic deans seldom use citation counts in assessing individual performance (see survey results in Chapter One). Certainly the counts can now be easily obtained. The *Science Citations Index* refers to journals and books in the natural science fields and the *Social Science Citations Index* provides references to journals (not books) in history and the social sciences. No index exists in the humanities. It frequently takes up to two years before a piece appears in a journal and a few years more before citations are published and can be indexed—a length of time that may make citations indexes inappropriate for tenure decisions or lower-level promotions. Since tenure decisions are often made within six years, time may not be sufficient for citations of the work of recent Ph.D.s to be indexed, but for higher level promotions more time has elapsed and a citations count could be valuable information. Many institutions require a national or international reputation in one's field for advancement to full professorship, and citation counts could shed light on that status. Clark (1957) found, for example, that choices made by a panel of experts in psychology correlated highest with the number of journal citations for an individual psychologist. Menard (1971) argues that citations are especially useful in comparing people working in the same subfield because differences in growth rate and other factors are less critical. In spite of their limitations, citation counts appear to be one of the better objective indicators of research visibility and value.

Another way of accounting for quality in publications is to give extra weight to articles in highly reputable journals, under the assumption that such articles were more expertly reviewed and meet higher standards than articles in lesser journals. Refereed journals could also be assumed to publish higher quality articles than unrefereed journals and thus deserve additional emphasis. In some disciplines, department members may be able to agree on categories of quality among journals in their field.

Should the Evaluation of Research Vary by Discipline? Because publication rates and patterns vary by disciplines, faculty members in different academic areas would be evaluated more fairly if these differences were taken into account. Specifically, teachers in the natural sciences publish more journal articles early in their careers than do teachers in the humanities or social sciences. Exhibit 18, based on a sample of teachers who had used Educational Testing Service's Student Instructional Report in recent years and had completed an instructor's "Cover Sheet" questionnaire, illustrates this clearly. The median number of journal articles for natural science teachers during their first six years of experience is over two, while the median for social science and humanities teachers during the same period is close to one and a half articles. During the first twelve years of experience, natural science teachers tend to produce more articles than either the humanities or social science teachers, but after then the picture changes: those in the humanities and social science publish slightly more than teachers of natural science, although all three groups publish less after twenty years of experience than at any time previously.

If a college or university compared teachers on the productivity of journal articles regardless of discipline, it is likely that natural scientists would have a decided edge during the early years. Research and scholarship in the humanities and social sciences are generally slower to develop compared with the natural sciences; moreover, they more frequently result in book publication. For this reason, departments that emphasize research in the humanities and social sciences put more weight on the publication of books than do natural science departments, as Centra (1977a) found in the survey of department heads (reported in Chapter One). Journal articles and grants received

Exhibit 18. Median Number of Publications During Most Recent Five-Year Period for Faculty Members at Four-Year Colleges and Universities

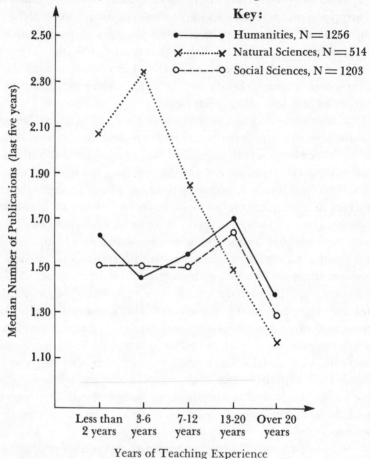

Key:

●———● Humanities, N = 1256
✗·········✗ Natural Sciences, N = 514
○––––○ Social Sciences, N = 1203

Years of Teaching Experience

are especially critical to the evaluation of natural science faculty members.

How Can Student Advising Be Assessed?

Prior to the rapid growth in higher education a few decades ago, student advising was the sole province of the faculty. But as institutions grew and became more heterogeneous in their offerings and in the students attending, alternative sources of advising have emerged. At large institutions, counseling centers staffed by professionals trained in educational and psychological counseling help students with vocational and personal concerns; academic advising is carried out in some departments by selected faculty members given reduced teaching loads or by trained professionals. Yet it is still true that on many campuses academic advising is the responsibility of the entire teaching staff.

In general, smaller colleges tend to rely on the teaching faculty; larger institutions use both faculty and professional advisers or counselors. Colleges within universities often vary in their approaches. At one university, for example, the business college employs trained graduate students, the college of education has a centralized unit staffed by trained advisers for freshmen and sophomore majors while the teaching faculty advises upper-class students, and the arts and letters college uses specialists with each department. In addition, students at this institution can go to the university counseling center for career or personal advice, or they may be referred to the center by their adviser. The four most prevalent approaches among community colleges are, in order of frequency: instructor-counselor, with the instructor doing most of the advising and the counselor having limited involvement; counselor-instructor, a reverse of the first approach; counselors only; and instructors only (O'Banion, Fordyce, and Goodwin, 1972).

Who does the advising is probably less critical than that individual's knowledge and commitment to advisement. A faculty member's commitment will in turn largely depend on the institution's expectations and—most important—on whether conscientious and effective advisement is recognized and rewarded. Criteria for judging advisers should be established and made known; a fair and systematic evaluation system should then be implemented. This system can be used to improve advisement and to reward individual effort.

Some of the basic criteria for effective advisement include (1) adviser knowledge of curricular requirements and college policies and procedures (for example, does the adviser provide adequate guidance in course offerings, prerequisites, major requirements, drop and add procedures, and the like); (2) adviser availability (office hours kept as posted, other meeting times arranged if needed, necessary time willingly taken with advisees); and (3) adviser acquaintance with other advisory and support services on campus such as financial aid, personal counseling, and career assistance (in order to refer students for help in these areas at the appropriate time).

These would generally be considered the minimal duties of an adviser. Kramer and Gardner (1977) use the phrase "informational advising" in referring to these basic duties and estimate that 80 percent of the advising in colleges and universities is at this level. Moreover, they add, information is to advising as knowledge of subject matter is to teaching. To gain credibility with students, advisers must have command of their basic information. Most institutions and departments hope that their faculty advisers will perform adequately at this level, but some colleges would like them to do much more. They expect faculty members to know advisees well enough to help them plan an educationally sound program and to assist students in developing career plans. They also expect that advisers will meet regularly with students to discuss problems and progress, both academic and personal. These may be institutions that believe that the teaching faculty should be involved in developing the "whole" student, or they may be institutions without the financial resources to hire counselors and similar specialists. Faculty members who are expected to perform these functions effectively should receive some training; they would not have been prepared for this in graduate school.

As noted earlier, some departments identify one or two faculty members or specialists to carry the advising load for the entire department, freeing others for teaching and research. In determining workload, one suggestion is that twenty advisees are equal to one credit-hour teaching load. This assumes that the average faculty member spends two hours per week for each credit hour of teaching, and thus allows approximately an hour and a half per semester for each advisee. At the University of Kansas, career advisement is facilitated by making known the specific faculty member in a department who can best provide information on future employment possibilities and on training requirements. These names are listed by field or department in a manual so that advisers and counselors are able to refer students to particular people for additional current career information in a given field (O'Neil and others, 1978).

How Should Advisers Be Evaluated? Mayhew (1969) argues that the skills and attitudes demanded by advising are different from those of teaching. While teachers inject their personalities into instruction, advisers must subdue their personal impact. The subject matter and the teacher's objectives are important to teaching; in an advising relationship, the student and his goals are critical. In teaching, the instructor is less passive and less subtle than is needed in the more intimate advisory role. In short, like teaching and research, advising involves different—although at times overlapping—abilities on the part of a faculty member. Being effective in one role does not guarantee acceptable performance in another.

Are faculty members able to evaluate their own effectiveness as an adviser? Probably not. According to one study (Grites, 1974), adviser self-perceptions differ from student perceptions of the adviser's effectiveness. As with the self-perception that faculty members have of their teaching ability, advisers tend to see themselves as more effective than do their advisees. Clearly, then, adviser self-assessments do not provide sufficient information, especially if the results are used to determine rewards.

Department chairmen and deans may hear about inadequate advising through dissatisfied students who complain that advisers have failed to meet with them or that they are unaware of basic procedural information that the students need. A more systematic approach has the students respond periodically to a questionnaire dealing with the performance of their adviser. The dimensions that students rate will depend on the advisement philosophy of the institution or department. At the very least, statements relating to the three minimal criteria mentioned earlier (so-called informational advising) should be included in the questionnaire. If the adviser is also expected to handle career and personal counseling, then the rating form should reflect these areas as well.

Examples of adviser rating forms appear as Exhibits 19 and 20. The Colorado State University evaluation form (Exhibit 19) is a preliminary instrument designed for university-wide use. It was developed primarily for undergraduate student advisees and emphasizes informational advising. As question 7 indicates, the university has other offices that provide additional counseling assistance to students. Questions 12 and 13 provide overall or global judgments about the adviser and might be particularly relevant for administrative purposes. Item 14, which asks students about their need for advice, helps

Exhibit 19. Colorado State University Academic Advising Review

COLLEGE_____   Code: _____
MAJOR   _____   Code: _____
ADVISER _____   Code: _____

Colorado State University Academic Advising Review

Instructions: This review allows you to express anonymously your reactions to your adviser and the advising process. Indicate your reactions to the statements by putting the appropriate number in the blank to the right of each question.

Response Key: 1–Strongly agree 2–Agree 3–Disagree 4–Strongly disagree 5–Not applicable

Section I.

1. My adviser knows me well enough to be perceptive of my individual needs and how they influence my academic goals. _____
2. My adviser explains the requirements in my major to show the relevance of all required and/or recommended courses and how they will affect my educational goals. _____
3. My adviser provides me with information about the limitations, alternatives, and consequences of the major that I am presently following, such as: Is a graduate degree necessary? Are there jobs in this area? _____
4. My adviser helps me correlate my choice of electives with my long-range objectives and the requirements in my major. My adviser helps me make substitutions and exercise options whenever appropriate. _____
5. My adviser helps me figure out my schedule to meet both my immediate and my long-range objectives. _____
6. My adviser helps me in assessing my progress toward my degree so that we can work out the problem areas that arise. _____
7. My adviser is informed about other advisory and professional service personnel at CSU (Office of Academic Advising, Counseling Center, Career Service) where I could get additional assistance if I needed it. _____
8. I like the procedure that my adviser uses in arranging my meeting(s) with him/her. _____
9. My adviser sets aside adequate time each quarter to talk with me and advise me about my major, changes in program, and so on. _____
10. My adviser is willing to see me at least one to two times each quarter. _____
11. My relationship with my adviser is businesslike but friendly. _____
12. Overall, I am generally satisfied with my adviser and the advising I have received. _____
13. Generally, the information I have received from my adviser has been accurate. _____

Exhibit 19. (continued)

Section II.

14. I really don't feel that I need formal advising.   _____
15. My adviser should know me personally because I have given
    him/her sufficient opportunity to do so.   _____
16. I keep my adviser informed of all the changes in my schedule
    that I have made whenever I have had to add/drop a course
    or withdraw from a course.   _____
17. I keep my own copy of the curriculum checksheet so that I
    can assess my progress toward a degree.   _____
18. I have found other faculty members who have been more
    helpful to me than my assigned adviser.   _____

Note: For the following questions, put the number of the appropriate response
in the blank.

19. Meetings with my adviser are generally arranged at my
    initiative. 1) Yes 2) No   _____
20. I have failed to meet with my adviser at a pre-arranged time.
    1) Yes 2) No (If Yes, about how many times? ____)   _____
21. My adviser has failed to keep pre-arranged appointments.
    1) Yes 2) No (If Yes, about how many times? ____)   _____
22. My adviser has also been an instructor in at least one of my
    classes. 1) Yes 2) No   _____

Section III.

23. My class standing is 1)Freshman 2) Sophomore 3)Junior
    4) Senior 5) Graduate 6) Other   _____
24. My overall grade point average is 1) Under 2.00 2) 2.01-2.50
    3) 2.51-3.00 4) Above 3.00 5) No CSU gpa yet   _____
25. How many advisers have you had at Colorado State
    University? 1) One 2) Two 3) Three 4) Four or more   _____
26. How many times have you changed your major? 1) One
    2) Two 3) Three or more   _____
27. How long have you had your present adviser? 1) One quarter
    2) Two or three quarters 3) Four to six quarters 4) More
    than six quarters   _____
28. On the average, how many times do you try to see your
    adviser each quarter? 1) Never 2) 1-2 times 3) 3-4 times
    4) More than 4 times   _____
29. Do you feel definite about what you intend to do upon
    graduation or upon leaving CSU? 1) Quite certain
    2) Somewhat certain 3) Uncertain   _____
30. Are you a transfer student? 1) Yes 2) No   _____

Please put any additional comments you wish to make on the back of this
sheet.

Thank you.

Exhibit 20. Ohio State University Annual Student Evaluation of University College Advisers

Time Needed: 5 Minutes

University College asks for your help in assessing its advisement services

I.   Use pen *or* pencil. Print Autumn Qtr. '73 adviser's name here _____
     (Complete evaluation only if you were enrolled at OSU Autumn Qtr. '73.)
II. After every item, mark an X in the box containing your answer.
III. Complete evaluation *before* leaving Ballroom, and drop it into a marked carton at the exits!
     (Or turn it in when you turn in your registration form.)

1. Autumn Qtr. '73 CAP area: ADM AGR AHR AMP ART ASC DEN DHY EDU ENG GBC HEC MED MUS NRE NUR OPT PHR SWK VME   1

2. Number of quarters enrolled in University College (include current qtr.): 1 2 3 4 5 more   2

3. Cumulative grade point average: none 0.00-0.99 1.00-1.99 2.00-2.49 2.50-2.99 3.00-3.49 3.50-4.00   3

4. Number of CAP areas in which you have been enrolled (include current qtr.): 1 2 3 4 more   4

5. Number of University College advisers to whom you have been assigned (include current qtr.): 1 2 3 4 more   5

6. Class rank during Autumn Qtr. '73: freshman sophomore junior other   6

7. Job status during Autumn Qtr. '73: unemployed 1–10 hrs./wk. 11–20 hrs./wk. 21–30 hrs./wk. more   7

8. Course credit hours during Autumn Qtr. '73: 1–3 4–6 7–12 13–15 16–18 more   8

9. Residence during Autumn Quarter '73: home res. hall apt. frat./sor. other   9

10. Did you enter Ohio State as a transfer student? yes no   10

11. Number of conferences by appointment with your adviser during Autumn Qtr. '73: 0 1 2 3 4 more   11

0 1 2 3 4 more   12

13. Number of "drop-in" conferences with your adviser during Autumn Qtr. '73:

0 1 2 3 ·4 more

	yes	no	NBJ[a]	
14. My adviser was usually accessible during the busiest periods of Autumn Qtr. '73.	yes	no	NBJ	14
15. At other times, during his office hours, it was fairly easy to contact him.	yes	no	NBJ	15
16. My adviser kept appointments at or very close to scheduled times.	yes	no	NBJ	16
17. During these appointments there was enough time for my questions to be discussed fully.	yes	no	NBJ	17
18. I felt at ease talking with my adviser.	yes	no	NBJ	18
19. I could rely on the accuracy of the information my adviser gave me.	yes	no	NBJ	19
20. In matters requiring sound judgment, I have found my adviser's opinions to be of value.	yes	no	NBJ	20

Regarding ACADEMIC matters, my adviser knew about and was willing to help with:

21. required courses and program/major alternatives in my CAP area.	yes	no	NBJ	21
22. the process of deciding my program/major.	yes	no	NBJ	22
23. requirements for transfer from University College to the degree unit I've chosen.	yes	no	NBJ	23
24. long-range planning of my program according to requirements for graduation.	yes	no	NBJ	24
25. effects on my program of changing my schedule.	yes	no	NBJ	25
26. ways of resolving problems which affect my academic performance.	yes	no	NBJ	26

Regarding PROCEDURAL matters, my adviser helped me to become informed about:

27. how to plan, request, and/or change my class schedule.	yes	no	NBJ	27
28. university and college deadlines.	yes	no	NBJ	28
29. interpretation of college bulletins and other university publications.	yes	no	NBJ	29
30. ways to make effective use of University channels in solving unusual problems:	yes	no	NBJ	30

31. My adviser referred me to other persons for additional assistance when appropriate.	yes	no	NBJ	31
32. My adviser discussed student services (library, counseling, financial, tutoring, cultural, and so on).	yes	no	NBJ	32
33. My adviser discussed career opportunities for which I can prepare.	yes	no	NBJ	33
34. My adviser discussed the Code of Student Rights and Responsibilities.	yes	no	NBJ	34

35. All things considered, my adviser did a very good job.	yes	no	NBJ	35

If you wish, please write additional comments concerning your adviser on the back of this sheet.

[a]No Basis for Judgment

to determine whether poor advising may be due to an uncooperative student. Students also have a responsibility to keep their advisers informed about course changes and to take the initiative in seeking help when needed. Both of these concerns are reflected in the form.

The Ohio State University evaluation form (Exhibit 20) was used in University College during 1973-74. Judging from one or two of the items, advisers are expected to perform some general and career counseling. Item 26, for example, states: "My adviser knew about and was willing to help with ways of resolving problems which affect my academic performance." But the vast majority of the items deal with adviser availability, knowledge of academic and procedural matters, and acquaintance with other student services on campus. In addition to asking students to give their reactions to their advisers, the Ohio State form also inquired about the number of contacts or conferences between student and adviser (items 11-13); this kind of descriptive information adds a quantitative as well as a qualitative dimension to evaluation results.

The Kansas State University Center for Faculty Evaluation and Development has developed an Advisory Survey Form consisting of fifty-two items for which they provide computer processing. Assessments are provided for three outcome categories: student course selection, career choice, and personal problem solving. Specific behaviors of the adviser which relate to these outcomes are also included, along with student expectations about advice.

Are Other Methods Useful? Student reports or evaluations of advising can be used to improve the individual performance of advisers as well as to identify aspects of advising that need general buttressing. After obtaining results from a large number of advisers, for example, it may be apparent that many are unfamiliar with other advisory or support services on campus. Workshops could be offered to acquaint faculty members with such services. Periodic assessments give institutions an opportunity to monitor advising while indicating to faculty members that the institution sees advising as an important function. Including evaluations of advising in the reward structure makes this point even more emphatic.

In using student evaluations of advising for reward purposes, questions of their reliability and validity should be considered. To date there have been few studies of these issues. How many advisees need to provide evaluations in order to produce a reliable mean score for the adviser? If we can generalize from student evaluations of teaching, then it is likely that ratings by fifteen or more advisees would be desirable. Preferably, advisee ratings should also be collected for more than one semester in order to examine patterns of evaluation (as with evaluations of teaching), and students responding should not represent a biased sample for an adviser. All of these precautions are, of course, less critical if the results are used solely to improve advising.

As for the validity of advisee ratings, one analysis of the Kansas State form indicates that ratings by college administrators who manage or coordinate advising systems agree generally with ratings by student advisees (Brock, 1978). Whether good advisement, as judged by students, reduces student dropouts and is related to other objective criteria is a question for further study.

Other than student advisees, people in charge of the system may be in the best position to judge an individual adviser. In addition, objective information that provides unobtrusive measures of possible adviser effects should be considered. Do students meet their degree requirements without loss of time? Have proper sequences been followed? Are students' programs adequate for job or graduate school placement? How frequently do advisers refer students to other campus services? Is the student dropout rate low?

Assessing Public and Community Service

Public and community service is infrequently recognized and rewarded. A survey of department heads (Centra, 1977a) indicated that only 2 percent considered public and community service to be a critical factor in evaluating faculty members, while a third said it was not a factor at all. Most said it was a minor factor. Moreover, these proportions did not change when the department heads reported how faculty members should be evaluated.

Yet public service is indeed a major professional responsibility for some faculty members and their efforts should be assessed. The guidelines for promotion at one state university, for example, inform faculty members that contributions to the public service program of the university will be given as much weight as teaching and research if it is part of an individual's assigned duties. If institutions profess the importance of public service as part of their mission, they should be willing to recognize the efforts of their faculty members.

What Is Public or Community Service? The terms "public" and "community" service have generally the same meaning. Haberman and Quinn (1977, p. 140), after pointing out that there is little agreement as to what constitutes community service, list several criteria for community service activities. They include service to nonacademic community organizations and government agencies outside the university, contributing the individual's professional backgrounds and skills to government and community concerns, and advancing the ability of the university to relate teaching and research activities to community concerns.

Examples of community service activities are categorized by Haberman and Quinn into four levels. The first includes activities that last over at least one academic year with primary responsibility for such services as extensive consultation, developing a significant program, or coordinating a major research project. The second level requires involvement of a little less than a year and includes such services as assistance with workshops or supervision of projects. Third-level activities involve continued services with a particular agency for two to three months. The last level includes one-time activities calling for a few days of preparation, such as making public presentations or leading a discussion.

These levels will not apply to all institutions or departments. They serve as an example, however, which institutions may want to consider in adapting criteria to the various departments. It is unlikely, as Haberman and Quinn note, that any one system of categorization will be equitable for political scientists, artists, engineers, social workers, teacher educators, and other fields.

Dressel (1976) identifies three types of public service. The first type, which he calls "national missions," employs the agricultural extension model of the land-grant universities. Federal legislation has extended this model to business, industry, and urban problems, and colleges and universities are applying their expertise to solving problems in each of these areas.

A second type, continuing education, has gained renewed importance with the current concern for lifelong learning. Dressel includes in this category nondegree courses, workshops, seminars, and other instructional experiences for professionals and other adults. He prefers to view the credit courses offered off campus or to part-time students as an extension of the regular instructional program—as do most institutions (McCarthy, 1978). Such classes often are part of a teacher's regularly assigned teaching load and should be evaluated in the same way as other courses. As Haberman and Quinn (1977) argue, "teaching does not become transformed into community service because the teaching occurs in the evening or off-campus. The quality of teaching should be judged by peers and students on the same criteria wherever it occurs."

Dressel's third type of public service program is assistance to community groups. Depending on the specific needs of the group, faculty from an appropriate discipline might become involved in providing assistance.

How Should Public and Community Service Be Evaluated? A faculty member's annual report should include details on community service activities. Examples of proposals, reports, articles, and other supporting documents can be provided along with the individual's description of objectives, perceived outcomes, time involved, and remuneration received. Merely being involved in public or community service is not a sufficient indicator of effectiveness. Noncredit courses, workshops, and the like can be evaluated according to the number of people attracted to them and by student judgments concerning course content and teacher effectiveness. Less is known about the validity of such assessments, but they are likely to be subject to the same strengths and weaknesses discussed earlier regarding student ratings of traditional courses. If the information is applied to administrative decisions, it should be collected and interpreted with these limitations in mind. Colleagues in an appropriate field also can assess the materials and objectives of these courses.

Involvement in other types of service can in part be judged through comments by the agencies or firms involved and, as Dressel (1976) suggests, by grants or contracts for the extension or expansion of services. Preferably, and whenever possible, public service activities should also be assessed according to the extent to which the objectives of the programs have been accomplished.

—————————— *SEVEN* ——————————

Legal Considerations and Personnel Decisions

Administrators, faculty members, and others involved with personnel decisions should be aware of the legal implications of the assessment concerns with which this book deals. Awareness, of course, does not substitute for legal counsel. College officials should consult with attorneys when personnel policies are being formulated as well as when conflicts first arise. Legal advice at the early stages of a controversy can lead to a settlement or to a stronger case in court (Shur and LeBlanc, 1975). More important, consulting with legal advisers when personnel policies are being formed can minimize the number of potential grievance procedures and lawsuits.

Three major questions are discussed in this chapter: What legal principles should institutions consider in establishing procedures for faculty personnel decisions? What does the law say about assessment criteria? How have the courts viewed disputes over instruction and course content? The answers rely on past court decisions, some of which are limited in their applicability; only Supreme Court decisions are binding throughout the country. Our complex judicial system includes ten federal jurisdictions and fifty separate state court systems. A ruling in one locale may not apply in another, although the courts generally take into account decisions reached elsewhere. College officials in Ohio, particularly at state-supported institutions, are best guided by what the Ohio Supreme Court has said on the topic (Blumer, 1975).

Readers who want to learn about legal issues in higher education are referred to William Kaplin's volume, *The Law of Higher Education* (1978). This sourcebook is the basis for some of the material in this chapter. The quarterly briefs of selected court cases entitled *The College Administrator and the Courts* (Bickel and Brechner, 1978), also provide a useful update on important court cases.

What Legal Principles Should Institutions Consider in Establishing Procedures for Faculty Personnel Decisions?

At a minimum, public institutions must comply with constitutional due process in making faculty personnel decisions. Due process means following certain principles, such as providing faculty members with proper notice and an opportunity for a fair hearing. It is provided to faculty members as to all citizens under the Fourteenth Amendment, which provides that states shall not "deprive any person of life, liberty or property without due process of law." Although a literal interpretation of this amendment indicates that it is not binding on private institutions, such a conclusion is not entirely correct. There recently has been an expanding interpretation of the Fourteenth Amendment concept of "state action," especially within higher education (Ryskamp and Simon, 1975). Since most private colleges now receive large amounts of federal and state funding, few are wholly private. Under this expansion, the "property" and "liberty" interests under the Fourteenth Amendment may apply to private as well as public colleges and universities, and officials of private colleges will want to keep these in mind in developing their personnel procedures.

It is important to distinguish between *substantive* and *procedural* due process. The First and Fourteenth Amendments of the Constitution guarantee such substantive due process rights as freedom of speech, religion, and privacy. The Fourteenth Amendment guarantees procedural due process, which includes the right to notice of dismissal, a hearing, and in some instances a statement of the reasons for dismissal. An institution must grant the faculty member procedural safeguards whenever its personnel decision infringes on a property or liberty interest. Kaplin (1978, p. 138) adds that: "Decisions to terminate tenured faculty members or faculty members in mid-contract must always be accompanied by such safeguards, since such decisions always infringe property interests. Nonrenewal decisions may or may not require procedural safeguards, depending on whether they fall within the property and liberty guidelines."

Kaplin also reports (pp. 136–137): "Nonrenewal of a faculty appointment requires appropriate safeguards:

"1. if the existing rules, policies, or practices of the institution, or mutually 'explicit understandings' between the faculty member and the institution, support the faculty member's claim of entitlement to continued employment.

"2. the institution, in the course of nonrenewal, makes charges against the faculty member that could seriously damage his or her reputation, standing, or associations in the community.

"3. the nonrenewal imposes a 'stigma or other disability' on the faculty member that forecloses his freedom to take advantage of other employment opportunities."

Although a full-scale hearing is not required before the personnel decision is made, some courts have required a hearing before terminating a member's pay or other benefits. Additional requirements of due process, at least at the elementary and secondary school level, may include offering teachers help in improvement and giving them adequate time to correct their deficiencies (Programs of Continuing Education, 1978). Fair requirements such as these would foster teacher confidence in their institution. Establishing proper personnel procedures takes time and effort, but they can help an institution to avoid or correct mistaken assessments, protect the academic freedom of the faculty, and encourage the resolution of disputes through internal negotiation and conciliation rather than through the expensive, time-consuming, and adversarial processes of the courts (Kaplin, 1978). When effective personnel procedures exist, Kaplin points out, the courts have been inclined to require faculty members to exhaust those procedures before filing suit. If suit is brought, institutions are on firm legal ground if they have observed the procedural requirements. If they fail to comply with the procedures that they have specified, however, they are open to litigation. At one college, for example, the rules provide that both the division directors and the chairman discuss their recommendations with the faculty member and that recommendations be brought to the president's advisory committee on promotion and tenure. When the college departed from this written rule, the state supreme court ruled that the contractual relationship between the college and the affected faculty member had been violated. (*Nzomo* v. *Vermont State Colleges,* 385 A.2d 1079 Supreme Court of Vermont, 1978).

Paradoxically, if an institution's personnel procedures are vague or unspecified, it is more difficult for faculty members to challenge decisions on specific procedural grounds. In general, if specific procedural requirements can reasonably be construed as part of the faculty member's contract with the institution (the contract being anything from a brief formal notice of appointment to a lengthy collective bargaining agreement), the courts will usually require institutions to comply with these procedures (Kaplin, 1978).

The two landmark Supreme Court cases on constitutional due process for faculty members are *Board of Regents* v. *Roth* and *Perry* v. *Sindermann*. Both involved untenured faculty members at public institutions and both were decided in 1972. Roth completed a one-year contract at Wisconsin State University, Oshkosh, and was not rehired. Wisconsin law provides that teachers in any state university be hired for one-year terms and be eligible for tenure only after four years of continuous service. Roth was given no reason for nonrenewal nor any opportunity to challenge it in a hearing. He alleged that he was dismissed because he had criticized the university administration and claimed a violation of his freedom of speech. He also alleged that he was not given reasons for nonrenewal or a hearing, a violation of the due process clause of the Fourteenth Amendment. The Supreme Court reversed lower courts in ruling that the teacher's Fourteenth Amendment rights were not violated since he had no protected liberty or property interest; the institution was therefore not obligated to provide reasons for nonrenewal or a hearing. Concerning liberty interests, the court said that no charge had been made against Roth "that might seriously damage his standing and associations in his community." There had also been no suggestion that the state "imposed on him a stigma or other disability that foreclosed his freedom to take advantage of other employment activities." Concerning property interests, the court (408 U.S. at 578) said: "To have a property interest in a benefit, a person clearly must have more than an abstract need or desire for it. He must have more than a unilateral expectation of it. He must, instead, have a legitimate claim of entitlement to it."

Sindermann had been employed in the Texas public college system on a series of one-year contracts for ten consecutive years when the board elected not to rehire him. During his employment he was openly critical of the board of regents. No reasons were given for the nonrenewal of his contract nor was there an opportunity for a hearing. Unlike the *Roth* case, the Supreme Court ruled that the professor's claim to de facto tenure was genuine. The court found that an implied contract may have existed, since the tenure guidelines for the particular college and the state system pointed out that there is no tenure system but that "the college wishes the faculty member to feel that he has permanent tenure as long as his teaching services are satisfactory and as long as he displays a cooperative attitude toward his co-workers and his superiors." In light of the policies and practices of the institution, the court ruled that Professor Sindermann had a legitimate claim to loss of property interest. Although this did not entitle him to reinstatement, it did entitle him to an impartial hearing in which he could be informed of the grounds of his dismissal and could challenge their sufficiency.

A college that does not provide a hearing may not have to reinstate the faculty member if he or she had not acted equitably (*Skehan* v. *Board of Trustees of Bloomsburg State College*, 436, F. Supp. 657 M.D. Pa., 1977). Skehan, a nonrenewed faculty member, claimed that the institution had not complied with a college policy statement that provided for hearings in academic freedom cases. The lower court held that the teacher possessed a contractual right to the procedures provided in the college's policy statement. In spite of this violation, the U.S. District Court of Pennsylvania ruled that the university did not have to grant full reinstatement to Skehan because he refused to teach his classes and refused to comply with administrative directives. The court held that prospective reinstatement is an equitable remedy that should be applied only to those individuals who have themselves acted equitably (Bickel and Brechner, 1978).

Where a formal tenure process exists, a faculty member cannot rely on informal assurances of tenure. In the case of *Haimowitz* v. *U. of Nevada* (579, F.2d 526, United States Court of Appeals, Ninth Circuit, 1978), a faculty member had been employed at the institution for six years. He claimed de facto tenure or expectancy of continued employment because other faculty members in a position to influence his tenure vote had assured him that he would eventually receive tenure. The court said he had no right to rely on such assurances since the institution had a tenure system. "The entire thrust of formal tenure is to standardize the process of faculty selection and employment security. In other words, formal tenure regulations are designed to avoid the de facto tenure problems recognized in *Perry* (v. *Sindermann*)."

What Does the Law Say About Assessment Criteria?

Within broad limits, the courts are not interested in determining the particular methods of evaluation or the criteria that institutions might include in their guidelines. They do, however, expect the evidence obtained to be job related and nondiscriminatory. The procedures and criteria that most institutions publish as guidelines in making appointment and promotion decisions are generally considered part of the legal contract between the institution and the faculty member. Typically, this contract includes such documents as the faculty handbook and the college bylaws. In some instances, the guidelines prepared by the American Association of University Professors are incorporated in the contract. Examples of procedures and guidelines (contracts) are given in Chapter Eight.

Kaplin (1978, p. 129) points out that "courts are less likely to become involved in disputes concerning the *substance* of standards and criteria than in disputes over procedures for enforcing standards and criteria." In the case of *Brouillette* v. *Board of Directors of Merged Area IX* (519, F.2d 939, Seventh Circuit, 1976), for example, the court, in rejecting the claims of a community college teacher, noted that "such matters as the competence of teachers and the standards of its measurement are not, without more, matters of constitutional dimensions. They are peculiarly appropriate to state and local administration."

Although courts are not generally inclined to dictate what sources of information or types of ratings colleges should use to determine a faculty member's performance, there are at least two instances when they can become involved in disputes. The first is when the criteria are specified in the faculty contract and there is a dispute over the interpretation. Such disputes may be settled legally if the institution's internal grievance procedures fail to resolve them. If, for example, an institution's guidelines specify that teaching effectiveness will be judged by students, colleagues, and department chairman—and if these sources are not used—a faculty member may have the basis for a grievance. The second instance has become increasingly common; it exists when charges of unfair discrimination are brought against an institution under the various federal and state statutes. According to these statutes, any group or any individual within a group must be assessed for a job on the basis of qualities that are directly related to performance on that job. Federal or state agencies involved in enforcing the various civil rights statutes are concerned with any measure used in hiring, promotion, or dismissal. Such measures are not limited to tests but include performance appraisals through the use of observations and ratings, interviews, and similar types of information.

The most comprehensive of the federal employment discrimination statutes is Title VII of the Civil Rights Act of 1964, which states that: "(a) It shall be an unlawful employment practice for an employer—(1) to fail or refuse to hire or to discharge any individual, or otherwise to discriminate against any individual with respect to his compensation, terms, conditions, or privilege of employment, because of such individual's race, color, religion, sex or national origin; or (2) to limit, segregate, or classify his employees or applicants for employment in any way which would deprive or tend to deprive any individual of employment opportunities or otherwise adversely affect his status as an employee, because of such individual's race, color, religion, sex, or national origin."

Title VII does not prevent institutions from distinguishing among faculty members in determining salary, promotion, and tenure decisions as long as the distinctions "are not the result of an intention to discriminate because of race, color, religion, sex, or national origin." The Supreme Court expanded on the interpretation of Title VII in the *Griggs* v. *Duke Power Co.* case (401 U.S. 424 [1971]) by further prohibiting employment practices which were not job related. Thus, they ruled in part (p. 431) that "[I]f an employment practice which operates to exclude Negroes cannot be shown to be related to job performance, the practice is prohibited." The principle of job relatedness for employment practices was specifically endorsed by Congress a year later when it passed the Equal Employment Opportunity Act of 1972 which amended Title VII of the Civil Rights Act of 1964.

More recently, in *United Steelworkers of America* v. *Weber, et al.*, the Supreme Court ruled that Title VII does not prohibit race-conscious affirmative action plans. Although the case involved an on-the-job training program at an aluminum plant, it will probably affect hiring and employment practices in colleges and universities as well. The decision may be important in sex-bias cases as well since amendments to the Civil Rights Act included women in affirmative-action programs.

A recent court case in which a faculty member alleged a violation of Title VII after she failed to win a promotion and contract renewal is *Mosby* v. *Webster College,* (563 F.2d9d, United States Court of Appeals, Eighth Circuit, 1977). Mosby, a black female, was a nontenured associate professor at Webster College. The college gave a number of reasons for refusing to promote her, including student dissatisfaction with her teaching, her refusal to accept a sufficient number of student advisees, and her unwillingness to teach certain courses. Mosby claimed that the termination of her contract was motivated by consideration of her race and, specifically, that she had never been warned that any aspect of her teaching was unsatisfactory. The court agreed with the college that its decision not to award promotion or contract renewal was motivated by legitimate, performance-related reasons.

Another case in which the evidence from an institution's faculty evaluation system did not substantiate a faculty member's claim of sex discrimination was *Northern Illinois University* v. *Fair Employment Practices Commission* (374, N.E. 2d 748 Appellate Court of Illinois, Second District, 1978). Barbour, a female associate professor, alleged that Northern Illinois University's decision not to promote her or grant her additional salary increases was based on sex discrimination. The Appellate Court of Illinois reversed a state administrative body, the Fair Employment Practices Commission, and ruled that the teaching effectiveness, scholarly activities, and professional service of the faculty member were rated relatively low by her peers and students and that the university was justified in denying promotion and salary increases. The evaluation system at the university included student ratings of teaching effectiveness (although faculty could refuse to be evaluated by students), and peer ratings of teaching, research, and service. Elected representatives from the department's tenured faculty, along with the chairperson, comprised a committee that rated faculty on a zero to ten scale on each of the major activities, with teaching receiving 50 percent of the total weight. Barbour received a total rating of between 2.0 and 3.0, compared to department average of 5.6. Student evaluations of her teaching were also relatively low. Promotion to full professor, according to university policy, should be based on "significant professional recognition" in one's discipline and "demonstrated ability in teaching." The court rejected the contention that the rating system, because of its necessary subjectivity, was biased; instead, the court held that the system discriminated in favor of better teachers and "against those with lesser abilities, an entirely proper purpose unrelated to the sex of the teacher." Because of subjectivity in the rating system, the court conceded that—although it could be misused—there was no evidence that it had in fact been misused or that the rating discrepancy between Barbour and other faculty members was based on her sex.

Title VII is administered and enforced by the Equal Employment Opportunity Commission (EEOC), also created by the Civil Rights Act of 1964. The EEOC has implemented Title VII with a series of guidelines, the most recent published in August 1978 in conjunction with the Civil Service Commission, the Department of Labor, and the Department of Justice (*Uniform Guidelines on Employee Selection Procedures* 43, Federal Register 38290). The *Guidelines* provide basic information for college administrators and others in the public and private sectors who are involved in the selection and evaluation of staff members. They apply to all methods used to make personnel decisions including written tests, interviews, work samples, and performance ratings. These methods, because of their possible adverse effects on members of a race, sex, or ethnic group, should be "validated in accord with the *Guidelines,* or the user otherwise justifies them in accord with Federal Law" (see Sections 3 and 6, *Guidelines*). Although validation of evaluation procedures is always desirable, the *Guidelines* require users to produce evidence of validity only when the procedures adversely affect the opportunities of a race, sex, or ethnic group. If one of these groups received generally lower student ratings, for example, a faculty member might claim that the ratings unduly biased his opportunity for promotion; the institution might then have to demonstrate the validity of the ratings as an assessment of job performance.

What is acceptable validity in this or other faculty evaluation methods is still in question. However, administrators and their legal counsel will do well not to underestimate what the courts may require. The *Griggs* case and an important subsequent case, *Albermarle Paper Co.* v. *Moody,* 422 U.S. 405, (1975), caused consternation among industrial psychologists and their employers because of the exacting standards for validation that the courts established. The evidence that would be advanced to defend the validity of assessment methods should be considered as they are implemented. For example, in the *Northern Illinois University* sex discrimination case, the court held that the evaluation system, which included student and peer ratings, did distinguish good teachers from those with lesser ability. The validity and reliability of the various approaches to evaluating teaching have been discussed in other chapters of this book.

Although a court review of institutional procedures can be demanding, it is not unreasonable to expect that the criteria incorporated in an evaluation system be job related. There will be concerns about issues of validation, but it seems clear that rating scales or evaluation systems that include such criteria as the teacher's appearance, neatness, or sense of humor are questionable in any case.

Administrators need to be aware of the charges of employment discrimination that faculty members and government agencies can bring. To overcome these charges, they should be able to demonstrate that their procedures are adequate and that discrimination played no part in the decision. Increasingly, college administrators have relied on legal counsel to help formulate policies and to defend their decisions.

How Have the Courts Viewed Disputes over Instruction and Course Content?

The courts would prefer, as Kaplin (1978) points out, to have college administrators deal with faculty members in disputes over course content, teaching behavior, or classroom behavior. Courts have become involved in cases, however, where faculty members have claimed violations of their First Amendment freedom of speech rights. Although the courts view these rights as preeminent, in cases to date they have generally supported the institution.

In one case cited by Kaplin, for example, some parents and students complained about what they considered to be controversial comments and positions taken by a faculty member in class (*Hebrick* v. *Martin*, 480 F. 2d. 705, Sixth Circuit, 1973). The faculty member also used a nondirective style of teaching while the administration of the particular state university wanted her to use more traditional methods. The faculty member claimed that her First Amendment rights had been infringed, but the court viewed the case as a dispute over teaching methods, ruling (p. 709) that such rights do "not encompass the right of a nontenured teacher to have her teaching style insulated from review by her superiors when they determine whether she has merited tenured status just because her methods and philosophy are considered acceptable somewhere in the teaching profession."

Another case also involved a nontenured teacher at a state university. He was not rehired because he counseled students with his office door closed, seldom referred students to professional counselors, overemphasized sex in his health survey course, and belittled other staff members in discussions with students (*Clark* v. *Holmes*, 474 F. 2d 928, Seventh Circuit, 1972). The court disagreed that the faculty member's First Amendment rights had been violated by not being rehired. Disputes over course content were not matters of public concern, according to the court, and academic freedom is not a "license for uncontrolled expression at variance with established curricular contents."

Kaplin points out that the courts have been more receptive to faculty members' claims of First Amendment rights and academic freedom in more general instances than in classroom cases (as in criticizing the administration, *Smith* v. *Losee*, 485 F. 2d 234, Tenth Circuit, 1973; or in private activities, *Hander* v. *San Jacinto Junior College* 519, F. 2d 273, Fifth Circuit, 1975). Faculty members thus have much more freedom to express themselves beyond the classroom and to engage in whatever activities they choose. Generally, Kaplin (1978, p. 157) states, "whether in the classroom or out, administrative authority over teacher behavior or activities increases as the job-relatedness of the behavior or activities increases and as the adverseness of their impact on teaching performance or other institutional functions increases."

The import of this is that when an untenured faculty member engages in action protected by First Amendment rights (such as criticism of the administration) compared to "unprotected" activity (such as consistently missing classes), the institution will be on firmer legal grounds to deny renewal in the second instance than in the first.

Not all suits involving instruction or course content have been brought by faculty members. In one case, a student claimed that a required course did not match the college's catalogue description, lacked tests or grades, and was of minimal substance (*Ianello* v. *The University of Bridgeport;* see Carnegie Council on Policy Studies in Higher Education, 1979). The student lost the case because she failed to provide sufficient evidence to support her claims. Extreme violations by faculty members in their roles as teachers concern students, institutions, and—increasingly, it appears—the courts.

Conclusion

The judicial system is clearly not the arena to settle the numerous disputes that can arise over such academic matters as teacher behavior and course content. Nor have the courts been interested in dictating the specific methods that institutions should use to assess faculty members. The law is, however, very clear that colleges must use job-related and nondiscriminatory practices in making personnel decisions, and that they apply the principles of due process. No less should be required. Determining the effectiveness of people in their jobs is far from a perfect science, and it never will be; but by understanding the strengths and limitations of different methods of assessment and applying them equitably, faculty members and administrators will be better able to make fairer decisions and satisfy these legal requirements.

EIGHT

Assembling the Data and Making Decisions

A major theme of this book is that multiple sources of information should be used in evaluating faculty members, whether for administrative decisions or for the improvement of performance. In assessing teaching in particular, each of the methods discussed in the preceding chapters has its limitations as well as its unique contribution. Each is subject to misinterpretation or error; thus when using the information for tenure, promotion, or salary decisions it is important to compare one set of indicators with another in seeking convergence. The weight of the accumulated evidence will generally provide the basis for a fair decision. A variety of evaluation measures will also result in greater improvement in teaching because different sources will be effective with different types of teachers and will expose weaknesses in different areas of instruction. As one professor said, college teachers should give up the conceit that they are all born teachers.

This final chapter thus proposes a comprehensive model of instructional assessment—one that uses multiple sources—although it also discusses other approaches to the evaluation of instruction. The first half of the chapter reviews various methods of evaluating instruction and their potential for summative or formative use, as summarized in Exhibit 21. The latter half shows how the evidence accumulated regarding a faculty member's activities can be put together and reviewed for summative purposes with particular emphasis on assignment of faculty responsibilities, procedures used for review, and the role of administrators in the review process.

Assessing Teaching

Student Learning. Student learning is considered by some people to be the fairest and most objective method to assess teacher effectiveness. Information on what and how much students have learned in a course undoubtedly is critical for course and instructional improvement, but for summative purposes the practical and psychometric problems make interpretation of student learning difficult. These problems are discussed in detail in Chapter Five.

Basically, there are too many factors other than teacher competence that can affect end-of-course student examination results. The students' prior knowledge is one of these. At the beginning of most courses, students possess at least some of the knowledge and skills covered in the course. Testing students at the outset as well as at the conclusion of a course and comparing the resulting "gain" scores among teachers has statistical and other problems, not least of which is that the early test does not take into account all of the preexisting differences between students. Those differences (motivation level is one example) may be more critical than teacher performance.

The right situation would be one in which a number of faculty members are teaching different sections of a course with a common syllabus and a common final exam (teachers involved should not know the exact questions on the exam in order to avoid teaching directed to the test). Ideally, students should be assigned at random to each section to minimize preexisting differences between students that may significantly affect their performance, and no systematic bias should apply to the way students select a teacher or section. End-of-course class scores might then be compared among the teachers over several terms as one indication of teacher effectiveness. Needless

Exhibit 21. Assessment of Instruction or Course Effectiveness

Purpose of Evaluation

Method of Evaluation	Summative Evaluation (For Tenure, Salary, or Promotion Decisions)	Formative Evaluation (For Instructional or Course Improvement)
Student Learning (Assessment of student knowledge or performance)	Ideal method of assessment but difficult to apply: a. Need right situation b. Need proper controls	Very important a. For assessing progress b. For adjusting instruction
Student Ratings	Possibility of some bias, so need proper controls for collecting and interpreting. Use accumulated rating across courses and years.	Can be useful for some teachers. Changes may not be overwhelming. What to do about poor ratings not always evident.
Self-Evaluation	Self-ratings not very useful. Activities report essential, as are materials submitted by teacher.	Self-analysis can be useful. Video/audio feedback is helpful.
Colleague Ratings (Peer evaluations)	Ratings of classroom practices tend to be biased and unreliable. Peer evaluations of knowledge of subject, course outlines, texts, student performance could be useful, periodically.	Informal feedback, whether based on classroom visits or not, can be helpful. It depends largely on the skill and knowledge of the colleagues.
Alumni Ratings	Alumni ratings are difficult to obtain in a systematic and reliable manner. They correlate highly with ratings by current students, so in most instances, they would not add much new information.	Periodic alumni judgments about the curriculum and other college experiences can be useful in program and institutional evaluation.

to say, such situations are extremely rare in colleges and universities. Some people believe, however, that if criterion-referenced testing is used, it will be possible to judge teachers according to the proportion of students who reach a desirable level of performance, as is discussed later.

Evidence of what students are learning is most important for instructional and course improvement. An assessment of student progress during a course allows both teacher and student adjustments. This is especially critical when the subject matter is cumulative—when later material builds on earlier units. Although self-paced or individualized approaches to teaching rely heavily on formative evaluation, all teaching methods should incorporate it. Test results need to be considered not only at the total test level but at the single question level. As discussed in Chapter Five, tabulating responses across students on a given item or section of a test will indicate course areas requiring greater attention by the instructor, assuming the item was not ambiguous or misleading.

Student Ratings. When student ratings are used in tenure, promotion, or salary deliberations, several points should be considered. First, a sufficient and representative number of students should rate each course, and ratings for several courses—perhaps five or more—would provide the most dependable basis for making judgments about teacher effectiveness. A set of ratings over several classes will more fairly indicate the teacher's effect on students than will ratings for one or two courses; it will also show trends in performance. Second, although the ratings are generally free of consistent bias, a few course characteristics can apparently influence responses. Small classes usually get especially high ratings, possibly because they allow more individual student attention. Students also seem to rate elective courses or courses in the major area more highly than courses taken to fulfill a college requirement. How a course fits into the college curriculum might, therefore, be considered in interpreting ratings. Third, responses to global or overall items rather than to specific diagnostic items should be emphasized. Ratings of a teacher's overall effectiveness and student estimates of what they have learned are better indicators of actual student learning because they are not tied to a particular instructional style; some teaching methods work well for some teachers but not all, and the diagnostic items reflect teaching method. Fourth, because students are generally lenient in their judgments, student ratings may be misleading about the effectiveness of some teachers. McIntyre (1977) states, "While high student ratings do not guarantee that the teacher is effective, it will be a rare teacher who is effective and still receives low ratings."

Only some 12 percent of a national sample of almost 400,000 teachers received less than average ratings from students; the remainder were generally average, good, or excellent (Educational Testing Service, 1975). Local or national norms or comparison data can better distinguish between teachers within the average or above-average ranges by providing percentile information that allows comparisons with all other teachers in the groups. Some departments may object to a norm-referenced model based on local data because it pits one member against another and precludes the possibility of all teachers being judged as excellent. Thorne (in press) found this to be the case in helping a pharmacy school deal with the use of student ratings in tenure and promotion decisions. Ironically, he reports that some of those objecting had graded on a curve in their courses, yet did not see the contradiction. The faculty ultimately settled on a criterion model developed by having each faculty member indicate an unacceptable or inadequate level of instructor performance in a course. The resulting distribution for the sixteen faculty members was: one categorized as "below standard," eleven as "good," and four as "outstanding."

When student ratings are used for instructional improvement, the detailed diagnostic items and written comments provided by students can lead to changes for some teachers. These tend to be teachers who have learned something from students that they did not already know, who value student opinion, and who are motivated to improve. For other teachers, changes are unlikely even though they may be needed. The leniency in student ratings may, in fact, reinforce the inflated view held by some teachers about their teaching. Comparison data can help the individual teacher put rating results in better perspective, but the problem for many teachers is what to do about poor ratings. Programs and activities to help teachers strengthen particular aspects of teaching should be available at an institution; teaching improvement specialists and department chairmen might then use student ratings as a basis for counseling teachers into the appropriate activities. Other ways to increase the impact of ratings are discussed in Chapter Two.

A final important point: care should be taken to ensure that student ratings are not overused. Total and mandatory use of student ratings could easily lead to a point of diminishing returns for the costs involved and the benefits received. If students who are required to fill out a form in every course every term may understandably give haphazard responses, faculty members too will be less than enthusiastic about the excessive use of student ratings. Institutions should, as McIntyre (1977) suggests, develop sampling procedures that fit local circumstances and that seek from time to time to include all appropriate courses and instructors. For nontenured faculty members, however, more frequent collection of ratings is desirable if the results are to be used in tenure and promotion decisions.

Self-Evaluation. Teacher self-ratings—their own written or numerical evaluation of their teaching effectiveness—are not very useful for tenure and promotion decisions. Although some teachers are able to evaluate realistically their effectiveness, others have an inflated view and a few are overly modest or critical. Because of these variations, it is difficult to use self-evaluations fairly. Personal descriptions of teaching and other professional activities, on the other hand, are the crux of a summative evaluation. The materials or evidence that a teacher can submit to support teaching effectiveness include course objective and instructional activities; textbooks, handouts, reading and reference lists, and syllabi; lecture notes; assignments and projects; examinations and grading. Chapter Three contains lists of relevant questions under each of these five categories.

Both self-evaluation and self-analysis can be useful for instructional improvement, particularly when used in conjunction with other evaluations such as student ratings. Video and audio playbacks of teaching are stressful for some people, but they provide unique information that leads frequently to changes. Growth contracts or individual development plans integrate self-analysis and remediation; when properly employed, they can be helpful for both summative and formative purposes.

Colleague Ratings. Colleague ratings based primarily on classroom observation would not be reliable enough to use in making decisions on tenure and promotion—at least not without faculty members investing considerable time in class visitations or in training sessions to help them develop a common basis for judgments. Colleagues might better judge the substance of teaching than classroom activities. They would then inspect choice of text, course syllabus and objectives, reading lists and materials employed in instruction, assignments and examinations, and similar indicators of substance. The list of questions in Chapter Three provides a guide for colleague judgments in these areas. Colleagues are also in the best position to judge such characteristics as the extent to which a faculty member has mastered the discipline, keeps up to date in the field, and fulfills curriculum responsibilities.

For instructional or course improvement, colleague opinions and evaluations can be helpful, depending largely on the skill and knowledge of the colleagues involved. Classroom visits by colleagues followed by informal discussions have been useful as have other models to facilitate peer involvement in teaching improvement that are discussed in Chapter Four.

Ratings by alumni have been listed in Exhibit 21 as a source of information on teacher effectiveness. At first glance, alumni ratings are appealing. Alumni have a broader perspective from which to judge courses and teachers they have had and their ratings would seem to be relatively free of bias. But they are difficult to collect in a systematic and reliable manner. Locating a random sample of alumni and getting a high proportion to respond to requests for teacher evaluations on an ongoing basis takes a great deal of effort. Fortunately the high correlations between student and alumni ratings demonstrated in several studies indicate that current students provide essentially the same information. Special or difficult cases may warrant the collection of alumni judgments, however, and periodic reactions to the curriculum and other college experiences provided by alumni can be used in program and institutional evaluation.

An Example of the Comprehensive Model. The use of multiple methods to assess teaching as discussed above could be described as a comprehensive model of evaluation. The various methods provide different though somewhat overlapping kinds of information on teaching. The goal is to obtain some convergence with the gathered evidence. One institution's ad hoc committee on the evaluation of teaching recommends guidelines for evaluation which, in large part, reflect this comprehensive model. Its recommendations follow:

University policy on promotion and tenure states that teaching is the primary function of the faculty of this university. The policy also states that distinguished teaching is sufficient grounds for promotion to any rank. To ensure that university policy with respect to teaching is a practical reality rather than an empty platitude, it is essential that effective teaching be recognized and rewarded. Given this goal, the Ad Hoc Committee on the Evaluation of Teaching Effectiveness makes the following recommendations.

Recommendation I

A. Recommendations for promotions and tenure must be accompanied by a statement of teaching effectiveness which rests upon the systematic evaluation of teaching. It is the responsibility of Departments (or Schools) to devise evaluation procedures and collect systematic information. No single source of information is sufficient. As a minimum student evaluations, peer (colleague) evaluations and evaluations by Department Heads (or Deans) are required. At the option of the Department, self evaluations, alumni evaluations and measures of student learning may also be used. Self evaluations may serve as a valuable point of reference and as a means for organizing peer evaluations.

B. Departments (or Schools) are responsible for devising their own methods and procedures of evaluation. The following general guidelines should be followed: (1) Overly quantitative systems which reduce teaching effectiveness to a single number should be avoided. A profile which shows strengths and weaknesses should be sought; (2) Care should be taken to ensure that evaluation information is free of potential sources of contamination. Specifically, the faculty member being evaluated should not administer, collect, tabulate, or summarize student evaluations; (3) Departments should ensure that student ratings are not obtained at the expense of rigor and content. Departments should also exercise care and ensure that faculty desires for good student ratings do not contribute to grade inflation; (4) Care should be exercised in interpreting the information obtained through systematic evaluation. Judgments about teaching effectiveness should give due consideration to factors such as the level of a course, whether a course is elective or required and the environmental conditions under which the course is taught; (5) In preparing statements of teaching effectiveness to accompany recommendations for promotion and tenure, Departments should summarize *all* relevant evaluation information in an easily communicated form and forward it for review at the university level. Departments (or Schools) are not free to pick and choose and forward only information which reflects favorably on the instructor.

C. Department Heads (or Deans) must share the results of systematic evaluation with the affected faculty member. Preferably this should be done in the context of an annual review.

Recommendation II

A. When a faculty member's teaching and instructional effectiveness are thought to be genuinely distinguished and deserving of special attention in decisions regarding promotion and tenure, a more intensive and systematic peer review is recommended. The Department Head (or Dean) and affected faculty member should reach an agreement about the composition of a select group of faculty members who are best qualified to make judgments on such matters as: (1) The appropriateness of the intellectual level at which the class is conducted; (2) The appropriateness of course content and instructional materials; (3) The academic standards employed in evaluating student learning; (4) Other activities or materials designed to facilitate learning; (5) The question of what was actually learned in the classroom of the instructor.

B. The decision to invite systematic peer evaluation of presumed distinguished teaching should proceed only under conditions and circumstances that will lead to mutual acceptance of peer judgment based on that evaluation. The following are suggested as procedures for such evaluation: (1) Peers should agree to visit the classroom of the faculty member over a period of time that is mutually agreed upon as being a sufficient time sample, hopefully corresponding to a complete "unit of study" for the course; (2) Peers should agree to adequately familiarize themselves with the text and outside reading material that are required of the students during the period of observation, so as to be in a better position to make equitable judgments concerning the appropriateness of the intellectual level at which the class is being conducted, the fairness of the examinations and grading practices, and so on; (3) Peers should assess the criteria and standards used by the instructor in evaluating student learning. Specifically peers should review the completed and graded examinations of students as well as other graded course materials; (4) Student evaluations of instruction should be administered at the end of the specific period that faculty peers observe the instruction. This should permit the peers to determine to what extent, if any, student ratings were gained at the expense of rigor and content.

C. The Department Head (or Dean) in consultation with the peer evaluators and the senior faculty will determine whether they wish to recommend the faculty member for promotion and/or tenure with special emphasis on excellence in teaching. In making this decision all information obtained from the systematic evaluation as well as all other relevant information concerning the quality of the faculty performance should be weighed. If a decision to recommend promotion and/or tenure on the basis of distinguished teaching is made, then all evaluation information must be summarized in an easily communicated form and forwarded for review at the university level. It is emphasized that *all* information, including that which reflects negatively on the quality of teaching, must be summarized and sent forward. Departments (or Schools) are not free to pick and choose and forward only information which reflects favorably on the instructor.

D. Department Heads (or Deans) are not duty bound to agree to all requests for review of presumed distinguished teaching. The review process will consume substantial quantities of time, resources, and faculty energy. Departments (or Schools) have limited capacity to make such reviews. Department Heads (or Deans) must decide how many as well as which presumed distinguished teachers are to be reviewed. If a request for such review is turned down the Department Head should provide a written explanation of the reasons.

Recommendation III

If recommendation I is adopted it is essential that the University create avenues which systematically aid faculty members in improving their effectiveness. Such help should be extended only to faculty members requesting it. A university-wide Faculty Development Center and faculty development activities originating within the Schools and College are alternative ways of providing systematic aid to faculty. A study of the alternative means of implementing this recommendation should be carried out.

As a starting point, this committee's recommendations provide the various units of the institution with an excellent framework for looking at teacher effectiveness. A few of their guidelines and recommendations, however, require further clarification. They did not make clear in Recommendation 1 which colleagues will evaluate teaching and what they should focus on. Several options are discussed in Chapter Four, and the various schools or departments in an institution may opt for different ones. Because peer assessments of teaching are especially sensitive, peer review procedures should be flexible; the committee's recommendation for peer review was eventually modified so that each department could select its own approach.

Self-evaluations are also left undefined. Are they to be actual ratings or descriptions of teaching practices and evidence of effectiveness, as suggested in Chapter Three? The various evaluations suggested under Recommendation 1, moreover, would best be obtained for more than one course and over more than one semester for each teacher.

Recommendation 2 gives departments a procedure for evaluating and recommending distinguished teachers. The procedure, while time consuming, allows departments to recommend for promotion someone who is an outstanding teacher but whose research or service contributions may be only mediocre. At an institution where teaching is the primary function, this recommendation is certainly reasonable. So too is the third recommendation, which calls for systematic aid to faculty who want to improve their effectiveness.

The comprehensive model is an excellent framework for institutions and departments to use in establishing their own evaluation system, the specifics of which should be worked out by each institution—most likely by a representative committee that actively solicits suggestion from the total faculty. Public hearings and published minutes of the committee's deliberations will help keep people informed and will give faculty members the opportunity to participate in the development. Once a system is devised, the institution will occasionally have to make some adjustments that had not been anticipated.

An important consideration in an evaluation scheme is that the information needs to be collected on an ongoing basis rather than at a single time (such as just prior to a tenure decision). Faculty members' activities will be more fairly and reliably assessed when the data extend over a period of time; they will also have an opportunity to upgrade their performance before a final decision is made.

Some Other Approaches to Evaluating Instruction. Although multiple sources of information provide the best basis for evaluating instruction, some institutions may find it counterproductive to force acceptance for each source. Student ratings, for example, should not be used if they are totally unacceptable to the majority of the faculty or if student participation in the program is very poor. A college might better emphasize other methods of evaluating teaching until faculty support or student participation can be acquired; colleague or supervisor evaluation systems, for example, might be strengthened. Other approaches or modifications to instructional evaluation that colleges have adopted include individual development plans, placing the burden of proof on the individual faculty member, and student learning outcomes.

Individual development plans (or growth contracts) provide a means of integrating evaluation, analysis, and remediation of instruction at regular intervals. As discussed in Chapter Three, these plans can be used by both tenured and nontenured staff and include not only an assessment and analysis of instruction but of all responsibilities of faculty members. They can be used in making personnel decisions, in which case a dean or an immediate supervisor generally takes part in the procedure; or they can be used solely for development, in which case colleagues, students, and the department chairmen can be involved. In either case, it is an ongoing and flexible procedure that places major responsibility on the individual. And as with its counterpart for administrators—the management-by-objectives approach—the individual development plan is being used increasingly. Chapter Three suggests that the plans could supplement the comprehensive evaluation model by providing a development or improvement focus.

A second and somewhat related method is what might be termed the "burden of proof" approach. Some institutions do not have a continuous or systematic evaluation system but expect staff members to provide evidence of their effectiveness. Individuals might submit accumulated student ratings, videotapes of their teaching, evidence of student performance, colleague judgments, and whatever other evidence they choose to collect. The information is then used mainly for personnel decisions although it may, of course, suggest remedial activities as well. Institutions that have adopted this approach do not require any particular kind of information, but they may make available rating instruments, video equipment, or other aids. At one institution where this approach is used, faculty members frequently submit summaries of student ratings or written judgments by colleagues. The advantage is its voluntary and flexible nature; the major disadvantage is that the information may have been collected without proper controls and thus may not be reliable or valid. Moreover, failure to provide information often carries with it the presumption of ineffective performance—which may not be the case.

Using student learning outcomes as a measure of teacher effectiveness is usually found in institutions that employ criterion-referenced measurement of learning (or mastery learning, or a systems approach to instruction, or a competency-based curriculum). Certainly, however, there are many institutions that use criterion-referenced measurement without also using the results to evaluate individual teachers. Moomaw (1977) found it to be used more often in the performing arts and in vocational and technical programs than in traditional academic institutions or programs. The measurement requires faculty members to define specific instructional objectives and levels of performance for students; they are then rewarded according to the success rate of their students. At one two-year college, for example, promotions and salaries were determined according to the percentage of students who successfully completed a teacher's courses. Final exams were made up by a college examiner to whom each teacher submitted questions for consideration. Although this reduces the likelihood that teachers will teach to a specific set of test items to ensure favorable results, many of the shortcomings of employing student learning to assess teacher performance discussed in Chapter Five should be kept in mind. Teachers might, for example, manage to bring students to a "desirable" level of achievement by stressing easily attained, low-level objectives, or by stressing memorization rather than understanding. Judgments by colleagues of course objectives and tests could provide a check on some of these shortcomings.

Taking Faculty Workload into Account. Some institutions or departments may want to reward faculty for the quantity as well as the quality of their work. Past studies of faculty workload have emphasized how faculty members spent their time and, in particular, how much time went into their various professional activities. This information was provided by the faculty members themselves and was employed in institutional planning and to document for boards of control or legislatures how faculty resources were used (Stecklein, 1974). It would not make sense to use a faculty member's own time allocations as a basis for determining rewards since people work at different speeds.

Quantity of work is already a critical factor in the evaluation of research and service. Consider, for example, that the number of publications and the number of committees are generally taken into account. Much less frequently is quantity considered in assessing teaching performance. When large variations in teaching workloads exist, individuals with the extra load not only have greater responsibility but may receive poorer quality ratings because they are not able to spend as much time with individual students. Certainly faculty members should not be penalized as a result of heavy teaching loads or especially large classes. Quantity factors such as these should be taken into account in an overall assessment but should not outweigh quality judgments.

Buhl and Lane (1977) designed a procedure for a two-year technical college that integrates quantity and quality information but which puts much more weight on quantity. Their model for one division at the college consisted of points assigned to instructional and other responsibilities. Under instruction they included five specifics: number of contact hours, number of preparations, teaching evening or Saturday classes, class size, and new courses. Other responsibilities, which accounted for only one-fourth of the quantitative total, consisted of department/division committee work, club adviser, work on the departmental curriculum, recruiting and placement activity, attending workshops on teaching, preparing new courses, and attending professional workshops. The qualitative component for this division included student ratings of instruction, the number of courses which were "designed in conformity with some model described in the literature on teaching and learning," and documented evidence of exceptional performance in at least one area of institutional service. This qualitative component, however, was weighted much less than the quantitative one—teachers could add only one-seventh of the quantitative total by receiving top quality ratings. The instructional workload thus was by far the major factor in personnel evaluation, comprising over two-thirds of the total point count. Teachers with more contact hours and course preparations were in the best position for favorable overall evaluations, as were those who taught new courses, large classes, and evening or Saturday classes.

This model was apparently suitable for the two-year technical college that adopted it, but most departments or institutions might find it unacceptable because of the heavy emphasis on quantity. It would of course be possible to reduce to a more reasonable amount the weight given to quantity: someone who teaches several courses poorly should not be rewarded more than the teacher who does an excellent job with an average teaching load.

Reviewing the Evidence

For personnel decisions, a critical part of evaluation is how the evidence accumulated is to be put together and reviewed. This section discusses the assignment of faculty responsibilities, the review process, and the application of standards. Such issues as merit pay increases and the role of administrators in faculty assessment are also considered.

The Assignment of Responsibilities. There is no question that faculty members should know in advance exactly what their responsibilities are. These responsibilities are increasingly being spelled out to each individual. The 1978–81 agreement between the Board of Regents of the State University System of Florida and the United Faculty of Florida (the elected bargaining agent for the faculty) states that: "Employees shall be apprised in writing at the beginning of their employment and at the beginning of each year of employment thereafter, of the duties and responsibilities in teaching, research and other creative activities, service, and of any other specific duties and responsibilities assigned for that year" (Article 9.2, pp. 6–7). Article 10.5 of the agreement states further that "the annual performance evaluation shall be based upon assigned duties."

A critical aspect in the assignment of duties is that faculty members know the relative weight to be placed on each duty in personnel decisions. Too frequently lip service is paid to teaching when in reality research is rewarded. The weights can be determined in various ways. One is through institutionwide policy: faculty members throughout the institution are judged on the same responsibilities, such as 50 percent teaching and advising, 40 percent research or other creative activities, and 10 percent service. Instead of a specific weight, a range can be given for each responsibility; within that range, departments and individual faculty members establish their own emphasis. An individual "contract" can be established between the individual faculty member and a dean or department head regarding the relative emphasis to be given to each possible activity and what the conditions would be for promotion. This agreement may be reached annually or it may be a long-time understanding that specifies the primary responsibility of the faculty members along with expectations. If it is teaching, for example, the individual is assessed mainly as a teacher and evidence of superior teaching is expected.

Although institutions should and generally do provide individual and departmental flexibility in defining responsibilities, many publish expected levels of competency for promotion to each rank. At one research-oriented state university, for example, effective teaching is necessary for tenure but advancement to full professor requires a "national or international reputation in one's field" as a result of significant scholarship, creativity, public service, or professional activities. Candidates to the rank of associate professor are not expected to have reached the stature of full professor, but potential as demonstrated by a sense of "consistency, direction and growth" must be evident. How phrases such as these are translated into decisions has been discussed in previous chapters and is considered further below.

The Review Process

The procedure followed at one doctoral-level institution in the South is illustrated in Exhibit 22 (Southern Regional Education Board, 1977). As in most tenure and promotions decisions, the proposal is initiated at the department level. The candidate provides a dossier detailing background information and accomplishments. At this institution the department chairman's recommendation is supported by information from faculty members within the department and from other colleagues. The faculty is also involved in the procedure as members of the area advisory committee. These committees exist in each major area of the institution, their members appointed by the president from nominations made by the faculty senate. They may request an ad hoc committee appointed by the vice president to

Exhibit 22. Procedural Flow Chart for Academic Appointment, Promotion, Granting of Tenure, and Termination for the Division of Colleges and the Medical Center

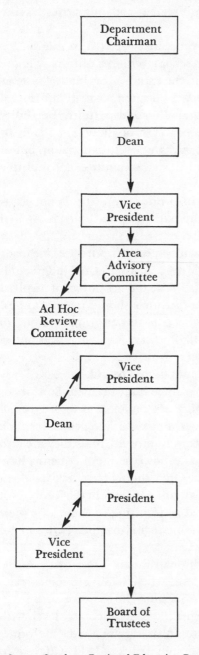

Department Chairman

1. Initiates the proposal
2. Provides appropriate vita including a list and sample of publications
3. Forwards recommendation to the appropriate dean with supporting data from tenured members and evidence of external consultation

Dean

1. Reviews the proposal and supporting data
2. Adds his endorsement or commentary and forwards the proposal to the appropriate vice president

Vice President

1. Reviews for completeness and forwards to the appropriate area committee

Area Advisory Committee

Ad Hoc Review Committee

1. Recommends approval or disapproval
2. May request ad hoc committee (appointed by vice president) for further evaluation
3. Forwards recommendation to appropriate vice president

Vice President

Dean

1. Reviews the proposal and all recommendations
2. Approves or disapproves the proposal
3. Advises dean of the action so the dean can respond prior to final action
4. Forwards recommendation to president
5. Maintains documentation file of all recommendations and actions

President

Vice President

1. Reviews the proposal and submits recommendation to the board of trustees for final action
2. Consults with appropriate vice president in cases where the vice president recommends contrary to the advice of the area committee

Board of Trustees

1. Takes final action (approves or disapproves the recommendation)

Source: Southern Regional Education Board, 1977.

make a further evaluation. Judgments at each level are added in written form to the dossier. Multiple reviews and judgments thus use the same evidence.

Rather than the uniform procedure depicted in Exhibit 22, variation allows departments and schools within a university to use their own criteria and standards. In their study of evaluation systems in the South, The Southern Regional Education Board (SREB) found some doctoral-level universities that allowed department flexibility and others that used the same procedures throughout. Smaller institutions, they noted, did not have as many levels of decision, but in most instances they also used faculty review committees and multiple reviews of the same evidence.

For annual salary reviews, institutions typically do not use as elaborate a procedure as that summarized in Exhibit 22. At that institution, for example, the department chairman and the dean make separate judgments about faculty members. Attempts are made to resolve any differences, with the dean making a final judgment if necessary. Decisions can be appealed, with the vice president involved at that point. All faculty review procedures should include appeal processes. The SREB study found that appeals were usually limited to questions of proper procedure rather than involving substantive issues.

Merit. Whether merit increases should be added to base salary increases is an issue that continues to be hotly debated. Bonuses or salary increases tied to performance are common to most types of employment. They are seen as a means of rewarding people for a job well done and of inspiring others to improve. Unless they are also seen as having been determined fairly, however, they frequently have a deleterious effect: people who feel they should have received them may decide to do only a minimal amount of work in the future. Not receiving merit pay is also viewed as insulting to those who view themselves as deserving; in effect the message is that their performance is unworthy and nonmeritorious.

Teacher's unions are traditionally against merit pay. At the elementary and secondary school level, where administrators exercise major control, bargaining agents question the basis for such judgments. Multiple judgments are more likely at the college level, with colleagues, students, and several administrators involved. One former president of the American Federation of Teachers (AFL-CIO) stated that merit may be all right for college and university professors if it is "based on faculty-determined principles and is distributed fairly" (Selden, 1978). If so, he thought that skimming off more than 5 or 6 percent of the salary settlement for merit increases would constitute a serious threat to faculty morale. He further speculated that awarding bonuses, which any faculty member might win in a given year, might be less repugnant to many people than merit money.

In passing out merit increases, some institutions have spent long hours determing small differences between staff members. If the final result is one teacher getting $43 more than another, it hardly seems worth the effort and most certainly is not worth the interpretation that teachers will make. As more teachers crowd into the upper ranks, colleges and universities seem to be increasingly turning to merit increases as a means of reward. When applied, the basis for decisions should be understood and accepted; fine distinctions and rewards should be avoided.

Applying Standards. During the review process, judgments can be made by quantifying the information obtained or by such general approaches as narrative or categorical summaries. Quantification entails the assignment of numerical values to the various activities, and ratings or points to performance on each activity. Specific point totals are usually prescribed for promotions or salary increases. Its appeal is that it appears to be an objective and clear way to make decisions; it may therefore seem more defensible in grievance procedures. A disadvantage is that in many activities a faculty member's effectiveness cannot be easily reduced to a number. Those that can, such as student ratings or numbers of publications, thus may be more influential than other evidence. Because quality is more difficult to assess, it may not be adequately taken into account. Moomaw (1977) found that doctoral-level institutions were less likely to use a quantitative approach than were four- and two-year colleges. Experience with the approach, however, is far from positive. One community college abandoned the system because it seemed to cause low faculty morale, and a four-year college found that faculty members took advantage of it by getting high rewards for unimportant behavior (Moomaw, 1977). In spite of the drawbacks, more institutions seem to be adopting a quantitative approach, probably because it is ostensibly objective.

Exhibit 23. Determining Overall Performance Rating

Professor A	Percent of Total Effort		Criterion Rating		Raw Score
1. Advising	10	×	6.3	=	63
2. Teaching	50	×	6.1	=	305
3. Faculty service	10	×	5.9	=	59
4. Administration	—				
5. The arts	—				
6. Professional status	10	×	4.9	=	49
7. Publications	10	×	4.3	=	43
8. Public service	10	×	4.9	=	49
9. Research	—				
	100%				568

$$568 \div 700 = .81$$

Source: Miller, 1972.

Examples of Systems. Miller (1972) prescribed a quantification system in his book on faculty evaluation. An example is provided in Exhibit 23. Professor A's professional load is dispersed across six of the nine categories, with half devoted to teaching. Each percentage is multiplied by criterion ratings, which can vary from a low of one to a high of seven. The faculty member's total score, 568, is divided by the total score possible, 700, for an 81 percent rating. Miller indicates that a five percentage-point difference or more between faculty members is indicative of better performance. It would also be possible to plot the criterion ratings for each activity on a seven-point continuum to produce a performance profile for the faculty member. How the ratings are determined is, of course, the critical part of this or any other system.

Arreola (1979) added to this system by also requiring faculty to indicate how much weight to place on each source of information in determining an overall evaluation. On teaching, for example, a faculty member may choose to be evaluated 70 percent by students, 10 percent by peers, 10 percent by self, and 10 percent by the department chairman. How to prevent faculty members from putting maximum weight on a source they can be certain will result in high ratings, such as self-ratings, is uncertain. Conversely, teachers may choose to put minimum weight on a valid source they feel certain will be negative. Each institution must also determine the basis for evaluations by each group.

The next step is to obtain numerical ratings from each source on a common numerical scale and to multiply these by the emphasis chosen for each source. On a five-point scale, for example, the ratings accumulated for teaching might result in the following: students 3, peers 4, self 5, and department chairman 3. Multiplying these by the weights assigned gives:

Students	3 x 70 percent	=	2.10
Peers	4 x 10 percent	=	.40
Self	5 x 10 percent	=	.50
Dept. Ch.	3 x 10 percent	=	.30
		Total	3.30

The composite rating for teaching, 3.30, is added to composite ratings for each other faculty activity determined in a like manner, and an overall composite rating is obtained by summing across the activities. Overall ratings for faculty members would be used in deciding on merit pay increases and other personnel decisions.

One of the most detailed quantification systems was suggested by Michael Scriven at the University of San Francisco. He developed a system in which points are accumulated for specific activities or evaluations. For example, teaching points could be accumulated as follows:

- Standard teaching load and number of preparations, satisfactory evaluation by students—5 points
- Extensive work on curriculum, revision on teaching methods—1 point
- Professional workshop for improving content or methods of teaching—1/2 point
- New course added after first year of appointment, each course —2 points   (plus four other listings)

These points are multiplied by quality and quantity indicators. Very low evaluations (by students and peers), for example, are worth a .5 "multiplier," while ratings in the top 10 percent result in a 1.5 multiplier. Student credit hours and the number of preparations per year are also converted to multipliers. Research and service activities have point values and multipliers delineated for them as well. For example a total of 10 points per year per area results in an "A" rating, while 5 points equals a "C." An increasing number of "A" ratings is needed for promotion to higher ranks.

Any quantitative system that is adopted by an institution will undoubtedly require more trial and error adjustment time than other approaches. The more specific they are, such as Scriven's, the more they will be subject to nitpicking and attempts to beat the system. The alternative approaches, which are more typically used in performance reviews, include narrative summaries and categorical descriptions. Department chairmen and administrators, after reviewing evidence provided by the candidate, by students, by colleagues, and by other sources, can summarize in their own words the candidate's performance in various areas and their recommendations. Categorical ratings or descriptors ("superior," "satisfactory," and "below average," or "meritorious," "satisfactory," and "needs improvement") are also used. These approaches do not preclude the use of quantitative information—average student ratings and the number of publications can still be considered, but they do allow decision makers to give deserved attention to the quality of publications, the quality of student learning, and other factors. They also can include a critical first step in evaluation—the relative emphasis (weight) placed on each responsibility of the faculty member should be understood at the outset. For example, it should be clear if 70 percent of a total assessment is to be based on research.

Administrator Role. Department heads and deans play a central part in putting together evaluation data. The role of the department head or chairperson in faculty evaluation includes providing information about a faculty member's performance (just as some colleagues may do) or integrating evidence from a variety of sources or often both. Department heads are frequently in a position to observe or monitor an individual's performance in several areas and to judge these in relation to what was expected of the individual. It remains for deans and other administrators, however, to consider the institution as a whole in acting on recommendations they receive. Granting tenure to someone who has performed competently but in a rapidly diminishing field, for example, would be difficult to defend.

Department head evaluations, unfortunately, are not always particularly helpful. Hoyt (1977) finds that many departments confuse evaluation with "eulogizing." Rather than make informative judgments about what has or has not been done, they provide what Hoyt describes as "pat 'em on the back comments." Other department heads confuse evaluation with description; they report how many committees faculty members serve on or what their student credit hour load totals. This is not enough. Department heads need information to appraise performance on committees or in courses. Hoyt also notes that the recommendation occasionally does not relate to the evaluation. A glowing assessment, for example, might be followed by a below average salary increment.

While considering the recommendations made by department heads and promotion committees, presidents, vice-presidents, and deans make independent judgments based on evidence accumulated in a faculty member's dossier. Although the candidate's performance level is of primary importance, these administrators must also take into account the well-being of the institution and other considerations. Dressel (1976) states that evaluation provides the basis for rational judgment in making decisions but frequently the choice also involves political, social, financial, and other considerations. Given the steady-state condition of higher education and the likelihood that many institutions are facing enrollment reductions, institutions must be careful about having a high proportion of their staff on tenure. Departments that are losing students are especially vulnerable to overstaffing. Given two candidates with apparently equal qualifications, therefore, deans must consider current and future course enrollments in deciding who should get limited tenure slots. Even if their evaluations were not exactly equal—if, for example, one was slightly stronger in research but both were good teachers—differences in course enrollments or versatility in subject matter can justify selecting the candidate on the basis of financial considerations.

The value of a candidate to an institution must be considered along with his or her merit (Scriven, 1978). Consider another example provided by Scriven that is currently common, that of a woman or minority candidate who had performed very well but is not quite as strong as a white male candidate in some areas. The department involved has very few women or minorities and the institution has been pressured to do more in affirmative action. On a more idealistic level, the institution may want to provide more role models for female or minority students. Weighing the value of the candidate to the institution can lead the dean to recommend the less worthy candidate. Such considerations undoubtedly already influence both selections and promotions, and the recent Supreme Court decision in the *Weber* case (see Chapter Seven) may encourage wider acceptance of them.

The institution's well-being is important in making faculty choices and its needs and values must be known to faculty members as well as the methods and criteria used to evaluate their activities. Beyond this the principles that have been espoused in this book are fundamental: base assessments on multiple sources of valid information, review the evidence at several levels, apply legal and ethical procedures, and use assessments to help people overcome weaknesses and build on strengths.

Appendix: Facts About Available Student Rating Instruments

Name: Instructional Assessment System (IAS)

Description: The IAS presently consists of six distinct forms, each tailored to provide diagnostic information for a broad course type (large lecture, small lecture-discussion, seminar, problem solving, skill acquisition, and quiz sections). Each form has three sections. Section 1 contains four global evaluative items whose major purpose is normative. Section 2 contains eleven items designed to provide diagnostic information. Section 3 contains seven items designed to provide information to students as well as being diagnostic. Sections 1 and 3 contain items common to all forms.

Note: Larry Braskamp, of the University of Illinois, collected the information in this appendix, which was provided by each contact person.

Contact: Gerald M. Gilmore

Educational Assessment Center

PB-30, University of Washington

Seattle, Washington 98195

Specimen Set: A booklet describing the system and containing sample forms and computer-generated results is available at no cost. Various statistical information is also available at no cost.

Availability: Institutions may purchase IAS forms alone or forms and processing services as well. Forms cost 2.5 cents each. Processing costs 5 cents per sheet scanned plus 75 cents per class surveyed. Additional reports of results cost 10 cents per class. All postage is also charged. Participating institution is responsible for distribution. The rates are the same regardless of the number of classes surveyed.

Name: Arizona Course/Instructor Evaluation Questionnaire (CIEQ)

Description: The CIEQ (a result of fourteen years of research and experience) was designed to collect student activities about a single course and enable instructors to collect evaluative information about their teaching. The form contains twenty-one standard items and space for forty-two additional diagnostic items which instructors can select from a 373-item catalogue. Interpretive information and normative comparisons (by rank of instructor, course level, department, college, institution, and required-elective status) are made available to each instructor so that he or she may determine the major area of strength and weakness in the course.

Contact: Lawrence M. Aleamoni, Director

Office of Instructional Research and Development

1325 E. Speedway Boulevard

University of Arizona

Tucson, Arizona 85721

Specimen Set: The instrument, report describing development, "Note to the Faculty," user materials, and Optional Item Catalogue are available at no cost.

Availability: Institutions may order the forms from the University of Arizona, return them for processing, and will receive two copies of the computerized report for each class section evaluated along with appropriate interpretive information. Local institutional norms will be provided when enough courses are evaluated. The cost is 20 cents per student questionnaire processed. Arrangements can be made to have the individual institution do their own processing.

Name: Student Instructional Report (SIR)

Description: The Student Instructional Report program includes a machine scorable answer sheet with thirty-nine questions, plus space for responses to ten additional questions that may be written locally. SIR covers such areas as: Instructor-Student Interaction, Tests and Exams, Course Organization, Student Interest, and Course Challenge. Student responses are presented as percent responding to each alternative to each item, item means, percentile equivalents of the means, and scores on six factors. Comparative data, based on national use of SIR, are available separately for two-year colleges and for four-year colleges and universities. Comparative data for approximately thirty academic disciplines are included.

Contact: Eldon Park or Nancy Beck
Student Instructional Report
Educational Testing Service
Princeton, New Jersey 08540

Specimen Set: Specimen set is available and includes a sample of the questionnaire, sample of the output, instructions for administering, *SIR Bulletin* (semiannual newsletter), order form, list of institutions that have used SIR, reports on development and uses of SIR, and on reliability and the factor structure ($4). Numerous research reports on utility, validity, and other issues are available as separate publications.

Availability: SIR is available to any institution or instructor wishing to use it. The questionnaire must be purchased from Educational Testing Service (ETS). Answer sheets are available for ETS scoring and reporting or for local scoring (Digetek [OpScan], IBM 1230, IBM 3881). ETS scoring and reporting results in three copies of a three-page report for each class or section in which SIR is administered. Reports are returned to the institution within three weeks of receipt of the completed answer sheets at ETS. Combined reports are available in combinations designated by the institution (departmental, total institutional, etc.).

    Costs   Answer sheets sold in packages of fifty.

Answer sheets ordered at one time: *Answer sheets scored at one time:*

First	20,000 (	1–20,000)	$.12		First	5,000 (	1– 5,000)	$.28
Next	20,000	(20,001–40,000)	$.10		Next	15,000 (	5,001–20,000)	$.24
Next	20,000	(40,001–60,000)	$.08		Next	20,000	(20,001–40,000)	$.22
Over	60,000	(60,001 +)	$.06		Next	20,000	(40,001–60,000)	$.20
					Over	60,000	(60,001 +)	$.18

There are cumulative price reductions for the answer sheets and scoring from one year to the next.

Name: Instructor and Course Evaluation System (ICES)
Description: ICES is a computer-based system whereby faculty can select items from a catalogue of over 400 items classified by content (course management, student outcomes, instructor characteristics and style, instructional environment, student preferences, and settings) and by specificity (global, general concept, and specific). Global and general concept items are normed by rank of instructor and required-elective status whereas specific (diagnostic) items, recommended for course improvement purposes, are not normed.
Contact: Dale C. Brandenburg, Coordinator
           Instructor and Course Evaluation
           307 Engineering Hall
           Urbana, Illinois 61801
Specimen Set: The catalogue, instrument, newsletters describing the rationale and suggested uses of ICES, and faculty users guide are available at no cost.
Availability: Institutions must order the student questionnaires from the University of Illinois, return them to that university for processing, and will receive two copies of a faculty report for each class section evaluated. Local institutional norms will be available for the three global items and items selected as part of an institutional core. The distribution and confidentiality of the faculty reports is at the discretion of the local institution. The cost is 18 cents per student questionnaire (orders of 5,000 or more) and 20 cents for orders of zero to 4,999 questionnaires. Catalogues are 15 cents and the remaining newsletters are 5 cents.

Name: Purdue's Cafeteria System

Description: Purdue's Cafeteria system consists of four FORTRAN computer programs, a 200-page operations manual, a computer-managed catalogue containing 200 diagnostic items, and a norm library. Cafeteria can be installed for local operation easily on virtually any computer having FORTRAN capability and it functions equally well as a sheet or card-based system. Cafeteria supports both administrative and instructional improvement processes.

Contact: J. O. Derry
MRC, ENAD 402
Purdue University
W. Lafayette, Indiana 47906

Specimen Set: Available.

Availability: Cafeteria was designed for installation at other institutions as a locally operated service. The system costs (one-time fee) $800 and is shipped, on source decks, within five working days of receipt of a purchase order. Institutions can also elect to contract evaluation services from Purdue's Measurement and Research Center (MRC). MRC provides all materials, and the cost is approximately 15 cents per student evaluator.

Name: Instructional Development and Effectiveness
Assessment (IDEA) System

Description: IDEA, used at over one hundred colleges and universities, has as its criterion of teaching effectiveness students' ratings of progress on course goals selected as important or essential by each course's instructor. No one model of effective teaching is implied. Beyond offering comparisons with all instructors in the comparison group (roughly 17,000 classes), comparisons are made with other courses of similar size in which students report similar levels of motivation. Where students report unsatisfactory progress on a teacher's goals and also report instructor's infrequent use of teaching methods which are related to their progress ratings, then the computer-prepared report identifies teaching strengths and weaknesses.

Contact: William Cashin
      Center for Faculty Evaluation and Development
      Kansas State University
      1627 Anderson Avenue, Box 3000
      Manhattan, Kansas 66502

Specimen Set: An information packet is available which includes all the forms, a sample IDEA report, and an interpretive guide. *One* specimen set is available at no cost. If multiple copies are ordered, there will be a charge of 45 cents for each set.

Availability: Institutions must order materials from the center, return them for computer processing, and will receive three copies of an IDEA report for each class and one interpretive guide. Instructional development written materials relating to the IDEA reports are available to institutions using IDEA. A fee schedule for IDEA is available from William Cashin. Institutions processing fifteen or more courses at one time will also receive an institutional summary compiling data from all courses.

Other Instruments/Systems: Departmental Evaluation of Chairperson Activities (DECA) uses the perceptions of chairperson and faculty members as a basis for identifying the importance and effectiveness of various administrative roles of the department head and for diagnosing strengths and weaknesses of the chairperson's administrative style. Contact William Cashin for more information regarding DECA.

Name: Student Instructional Rating System (SIRS)

Description: The Student Instructional Rating System is a means of collecting, analyzing, displaying, and interpreting student reactions to classroom instruction and course content. SIRS is designed to assess student reactions for feedback for instructional improvement, administrative decisions regarding instructors, and feedback to students to aid in selecting instructors. SIRS Level 1 assesses student attitudes toward aspects of instruction listed in the Michigan State University (MSU) Code of Teaching Responsibility. The computer norms are currently based on over 115,000 responses made over the last year. All instructors are to use Level 1 in all courses. SIRS Level 2 is selected by each teaching unit to reflect its goals. Results aid in improving instruction and in making administrative decisions. Level 3 is developed by students. Its use is voluntary and the results are published for use by students in selecting instructors and sections.

Contact: LeRoy A. Olson, Professor and Evaluation Consultant
         Learning and Evaluation Service
         Michigan State University
         East Lansing, Michigan 48824

Specimen Set: Available.

Availability: SIRS materials are not copyrighted and are available to other colleges and universities. Processing arrangements are made on an individual basis.

Name: Instructor-Designed Questionnaire (IDQ)

Description: The Center for Research on Learning and Teaching (CRLT) Instructor-Designed Questionnaires (IDQ) help college teachers collect student reactions to courses on individually designed evaluation forms. University of Michigan instructors using this approach to course evaluation first receive a catalogue consisting of 148 items. Each item is a statement about the results of teaching, about a teacher, or about some aspect of a course. The instructor indicates on a requisition form up to twenty-five items which express relevant concerns in his or her course. Individually designed questionnaires are then computer-printed. Finally, student responses to these questionnaires are processed by computer.

Contact: James A. Kulik
         Center for Research on Learning and Teaching
         109 E. Madison Street
         Ann Arbor, Michigan 48109

Specimen Set: A specimen set (including catalogue, requisition form, answer sheet, sample questionnaire, and sample report) is available without cost. Also available are two reports describing the rationale and use of the system.

Availability: Permission to reprint the item catalogue or parts of the catalogue is given on request. Processing of IDQ forms is currently available only to University of Michigan teachers.

Name: Student Perceptions of Teaching (SPOT)

Description: SPOT was developed to provide a flexible yet systematic procedure for gathering student opinions. The item pool of approximately 200 items is divided among eight general areas (course content, objectives, and structure; instructor's behavior; instructional methods and materials; outcomes of instruction; laboratory courses; clinical courses; production courses; and curriculum specific items). Normative data are provided to instructors based on three groups: baseline data from a representative sample of 189 classes, user data accumulated each semester based on all users of each item, and departmental data accumulated each semester.

Contact: Rina Weerts
            Evaluation and Examination Service
            University of Iowa
            300 Jefferson Building
            Iowa City, Iowa 52242

Specimen Set: The item pool, sample forms, and a series of reports on the development and use of the SPOT system, including research bulletins, are available at no cost.

Availability: Forms may be ordered at a cost of 5 cents per answer sheet. Processing will be done at the University of Iowa at 10 cents per answer sheet. Two copies of a summary report for each class will be returned with the original forms so that students may write comments comments on the back side of the forms. Normative data can be provided for the institution as a whole or for any subgroup, such as a department. Distribution of reports shall be designated by the local institution.

Name: (a) Student Opinion Survey: General
          (b) Student Opinion Survey: Supplement

Description: The Student Opinion Survey: General is a twenty-seven item rating scale which deals with course, instructor, and student characteristics important in many courses. It contains both general, summary items and more specific items. It also includes space for as many as eight additional items to be furnished by individual faculty. The Student Opinion Survey: Supplement covers much the same ground, but in essay format. Either or both of these forms may be used in a given course.

Contact: Kenneth O. Doyle, Jr.
            Measurement Services Center
            University of Minnesota
            9 Clarence Avenue SE
            Minneapolis, Minnesota 55414

Specimen Set: A limited supply of specimen sets is available without charge. When this supply is exhausted, specimen sets will be available at a nominal charge.

Availability: Both the Student Opinion Survey: General and the Student Opinion Survey: Supplement are available for use in other institutions. Please write for further information.

Name: Custom Questionnaires

Description: The Custom Questionnaires system enables individual faculty to tailor-make instructional evaluation questionnaires by choosing items from an extensive catalogue that includes about 350 items—some in ratings format, some in essay form; some very generally stated, some quite specific; some about course and instructor characteristics, some about student characteristics, some about student outcomes. The catalogue also contains a guide to selecting items. In addition to instructor-selected items, each custom questionnaire contains two summary rating items: How would you rate the overall teaching ability of this instructor? How much have you learned as a result of this course? Thus the system allows both individualization and comparability.

Contact: Kenneth O. Doyle, Jr.
      Measurement Services Center
      University of Minnesota
      9 Clarence Avenue SE
      Minneapolis, Minnesota 55414

Specimen Set: The Custom Questionnaire system is available for use in other institutions. Please write for further information.

Name: Endeavor Instructional Rating System (EIRS)

Description: EIRS is a computerized system based on a short questionnaire which can be administered in five to ten minutes. Item selection was determined on the basis of multiple factor-analyses of an earlier and much longer questionnaire. Research reports have been published in various professional journals providing information on the reliability and validity of individual items and on the effects of important variables such as class size, student grades, instructor rank, and mode of presentation. A scatterplot is provided for each department summarizing individual ratings on two global factors—pedagogical skill and rapport.

Contact: Peter W. Frey
        Department of Psychology
        Northwestern University
        Evanston, Illinois 60201

Specimen Set: Sample copies of the rating instrument, computer summary, and research reports are available upon request at no cost.

Availability: Institutions may order questionnaires from Endeavor Information Systems (EIS), 2407 Prospect Avenue, Evanston, Illinois 60201. The course designation and the instructor's name are printed on each form. After the forms are returned to EIS for processing, four copies of the summary for each class section are provided, including means, standard deviations, frequency distributions, and histogram displays for each course and a scatterplot for the department. Item norms are provided by departments and by divisions. Processing time is guaranteed to be less than fourteen days. The cost for the forms and the processing service is calculated as 16 cents each for the first 1,000 forms, 12 cents each for the next 3,000 forms, 10 cents each for the next 6,000 forms, and 9 cents each thereafter.

Name: Instructor and Course Evaluation (ICE)

Description: ICE is an OPSCAN form for student evaluations that is processed by FORTRAN programs on an IBM 370/158 to provide instructor summaries on fifty-six standard items and eighteen optional items. A computerized item bank is available to select optional items. Analyses provide university, college, and departmental deciles for each item (fifty-six) and four factors (two instructor and two course). Norms selected reflect course level and required/elective levels. Scores reflect items preselected as relevant by the instructor.

Contact: William G. Miller, Director
        Instructional Evaluation
        B-20 Woody Hall
        Southern Illinois University at
        Carbondale, Illinois 62901

Specimen Set: The instrument, sample output, and user's guide were made available in June 1978. Cost upon request.

Availability: Available to others utilizing SIU-C norms. Cost available upon request.

References

AAUP Bulletin. "Report on the Annual Survey of Faculty Compensation, 1977–78." *AAUP Bulletin,* 1978, *64* (3), 193–266.

Aleamoni, L. M. *The Usefulness of Student Evaluations in Improving College Teaching.* Urbana: Measurement and Research Division, Office of Instructional Resources, University of Illinois, 1974.

Aleamoni, L. M., and Yimer, M. "An Investigation of the Relationship Between Colleague Ratings, Student Ratings, Research Productivity, and Academic Rank in Rating Instructional Effectiveness." *Journal of Educational Psychology,* 1973, *64,* 274–277.

Arreola, R. A. "Essential Components of a Faculty Evaluation System." Tallahassee: Florida State University, 1979. (Mimeograph.)

"Assessment and Development of Tenured Faculty." Memo to the faculty from the Faculty Affairs Committee, Earlham College, May 2, 1975.

Astin, A. W. *The American Freshman: National Norms for Fall, 1977.* Washington, D.C. and Los Angeles: American Council on Education and Cooperative Institutional Research Program, University of California, 1978.

Astin, A. W., and Lee, C. B. T. "Current Practices in the Evaluation and Training of College Teachers." In C. B. T. Lee (Ed.), *Improv-*

ing College Teaching. Washington, D.C.: American Council on Education, 1967.

Batista, E. E., and Brandenburg, D. C. "The Instructor Self-Evaluation Form: Development and Validation of an Ipsative Forced-Choice Measure of Self-Perceived Faculty Performance." *Research in Higher Education,* in press.

Bausell, R. B., and Magoon, J. "Expected Grade in a Course, Grade Point Average, and Student Ratings of the Course and the Instructor." *Educational and Psychological Measurement,* 1972, *32,* 1013–1023.

Bayer, A. E. "Teaching Faculty in Academe: 1972–1973." *ACE Research Reports,* 1973, *8* (2).

Berquist, W. H., and Phillips, S. R. *A Handbook for Faculty Development. Vol. 2.* Washington, D.C.: Council for the Advancement of Small Colleges, 1977.

Bickel, R. D., and Brechner, J. A. (Eds.). *The College Administrator and the Courts.* Asheville, N.C.: College Administration Publications, 1978.

Blackburn, R. T., and Clark, M. J. "An Assessment of Faculty Performance: Some Correlates Between Administrators, Colleagues, Student, and Self-Ratings." *Sociology of Education,* 1975, *48,* 242–256.

Bloom, B. S. (Ed.). *Taxonomy of Educational Objectives. Vol. 1: Cognitive Domain.* New York: McKay, 1956.

Bloom, B. S., Hastings, J . T., and Madaus, G. F. *Handbook on Formative and Summative Evaluation of Student Learning.* New York: McGraw-Hill, 1971.

Blumer, D. H. "Some General Thoughts on Postsecondary Education and the Law." In D. H. Blumer (Ed.), *Legal Issues for Postsecondary Education.* Washington, D.C.: American Association of Community and Junior Colleges, 1975.

Borg, W. R. "The Minicourse as a Vehicle for Changing Teacher Behavior: A Three-Year Follow-Up Study." *Journal of Educational Psychology,* 1972, *63* (6), 572–579.

Borg, W. R., and others. *The Minicourse—A Microteaching Approach to Teacher Education.* Beverly Hills, Calif.: Macmillan Educational Services, 1970.

Boulding, K. B. "The Task of the Teacher in the Social Sciences." In W. H. Morris (Ed.), *Effective College Teaching.* Washington, D.C.: American Association for Higher Education, 1970.

Boyd, J. E., and Schietinger, E. G. *Faculty Evaluation Procedures in Southern Colleges and Universities.* Atlanta: Southern Regional Education Board, 1976.

Boyd, J. L., Jr., and Shimberg, B. *Handbook of Performance Testing: A Practical Guide for Test Makers.* Princeton, N.J.: Educational Testing Service, 1971.

Braskamp, L. A., and Caulley, D. "Student Rating and Instructor Self-Ratings and Their Relationship to Student Achievement." Urbana-Champaign: Measurement and Research Division, University of Illinois, 1978.

Briggs, D. "Influence of Handwriting on Assessment." *Educational Research,* 1970, *13*, 50–55.

Brock, S. C. "Measuring Faculty Advisor Effectiveness." Paper presented at the 2nd annual conference on Academic Advising, Center for Faculty Evaluation and Development, Kansas State University, Manhattan, Kans., 1978.

Buhl, L., and Lane, S. "A Quality and Quantity Model for Faculty Evaluation." In S. C. Scholl and S. C. Inglis (Eds.), *Teaching in Higher Education.* Columbus: Ohio Board of Regents, 1977.

Carnegie Commission on Higher Education. *A Classification of Institutions of Higher Education.* Berkeley, Calif.: Carnegie Commission on Higher Education, 1973.

Carnegie Council on Policy Studies in Higher Education. *Fair Practices in Higher Education: Rights and Responsibilities of Students and Their Colleges in a Period of Intensified Competition for Enrollments.* San Francisco: Jossey-Bass, 1979.

Carroll, J. B., and Sapon, S. M. *Modern Language Aptitude Test.* New York: Psychological Corporation, 1959.

Centra, J. A. *The Utility of Student Ratings for Instructional Improvement.* Project Report 72–16. Princeton, N.J.: Educational Testing Service, 1972.

Centra, J. A. "Effectiveness of Student Feedback in Modifying College Instruction." *Journal of Educational Psychology,* 1973a, *65* (3), 395–401.

Centra, J. A. "Self-Ratings of College Teachers: A Comparison with Student Ratings." *Journal of Educational Measurement,* 1973b, *10* (4), 287–295.

Centra, J. A. *Student Instructional Report Number 3: Item Reliabili-*

ties, the Factor Structure, Comparison with Alumni Ratings. Princeton, N.J.: Educational Testing Service, 1973c.

Centra, J. A. "The Relationship Between Student and Alumni Ratings of Teachers." *Educational and Psychological Measurement,* 1974, *34* (2), 321-326.

Centra, J. A. "Colleagues as Raters of Classroom Instruction." *Journal of Higher Education,* 1975, *46,* 327-337.

Centra, J. A. *Faculty Development Practices in U.S. Colleges and Universities.* Project Report 76-30. Princeton, N.J.: Educational Testing Service, 1976a.

Centra, J. A. "The Influence of Different Directions on Student Ratings of Instruction." *Journal of Educational Measurement,* 1976b, *13* (4), 277-282.

Centra, J. A. *How Universities Evaluate Faculty Performance: A Survey of Department Heads.* GREB Research Report No. 75-5bR. Princeton, N.J.: Educational Testing Service, 1977a.

Centra, J. A. "Student Ratings of Instruction and Their Relationship to Student Learning." *American Educational Research Journal,* 1977b, *14* (1), 17-24.

Centra, J. A., and Creech, F. R. *The Relationship Between Student, Teachers, and Course Characteristics and Student Ratings of Teacher Effectiveness.* Project Report 76-1. Princeton, N.J.: Educational Testing Service, 1976.

Centra, J. A., and Linn, R. L. "Student Points of View in Ratings of College Instruction." *Educational and Psychological Measurement,* 1976, *36,* 693-703.

Chase, C. I. "The Impact of Some Obvious Variables on Essay Test Scores." *Journal of Educational Measurement,* 1968, *5,* 315-318.

Choy, C. "The Relationship of College Teacher Effectiveness to Conceptual Systems Orientation and Perceptual Orientation." Unpublished doctoral dissertation, Department of Education, Colorado State College, 1969.

Clark, K. E. *America's Psychologists: A Survey of a Growing Profession.* Washington, D.C.: American Psychological Association, 1957.

Coffman, W. E. "Determining Students' Concepts of Effective Teaching from Their Ratings of Instructors." *Journal of Educational Psychology,* 1954, *45,* 277-285.

Cohen, A. M., and Brawer, F. B. *Measuring Faculty Performance.*

Washington, D.C.: ERIC Clearinghouse for Junior College Information/American Association of Junior Colleges, 1969.

Cohen, S. A., and Berger, W. G. "Dimensions of Students' Ratings of College Underlying Subsequent Achievement on Course Examinations." *Proceedings of the 78th Annual Convention of the American Psychological Association*, 1970, *5*, 605–606.

Cole, S., and Cole, J. R. "Scientific Output and Recognition: A Study in the Operation of the Reward System in Science." *American Sociological Review*, 1967, *32* (3), 377–399.

Costin, F., Greenough, W. T., and Menges, R. J. "Student Ratings of College Teaching: Reliability, Validity, and Usefulness." *Review of Educational Research*, 1971, *41* (5), 511–535.

Costin, F. "A Graduate Course in the Teaching of Psychology: Description and Evaluation." *Journal of Teacher Education*, 1968, *19*, 425–432.

Crane, D. "Scientists at Major and Minor Universities: A Study of Productivity and Recognition." *American Sociological Review*, 1965, *30*, 699–714.

Crittenden, K. S., Norr, J. L., and LeBailly, R. K. "Size of University Classes and Student Evaluations of Teaching." *Journal of Higher Education*, 1975, *4*, 461–470.

Diamond, N., Sharp, G., and Ory, J. C. *Improving Your Lecturing*. Urbana: Office of Instructional Resources, University of Illinois, 1978.

Diederich, P. B. *Short-Cut Statistics for Teacher-Made Tests*. Princeton, N.J.: Educational Testing Service, 1964.

Dowaliby, F. J., and Schumer, H. "Teacher-Centered Versus Student-Centered Mode of College Classroom Instruction as Related to Manifest Anxiety." *Journal of Educational Psychology*, 1973, *64* (2), 125–132.

Doyle, K. O., Jr. *Student Evaluation of Instruction*. Lexington, Mass.: Lexington Books, 1975.

Doyle, K. O., Jr., and Crichton, L. I. "Student, Peer, and Self-Evaluation of College Instruction." *Journal of Educational Psychology*, 1978, *70* (5), 815–826.

Doyle, K. O., Jr., and Webber, P. L. "Self-Ratings of College Instruction." Minneapolis: Measurement Services Center, University of Minnesota, 1978. (Mimeograph.)

Doyle, K. O., Jr., and Whitely, S. E. "Student Ratings as Criteria for Effective Teaching." *American Educational Research Journal*, 1974, *11* (3), 259–274.

Dressel, P. L. *Handbook of Academic Evaluation: Assessing Institutional Effectiveness, Student Progress, and Professional Performance for Decision Making in Higher Education.* San Francisco: Jossey-Bass, 1976.

Drucker, A. J., and Remmers, H. H. "Do Alumni and Students Differ in Their Attitudes Toward Instructors?" *Journal of Educational Psychology*, 1951, *42* (3), 129-143.

Eble, K. E. *Career Development of the Effective College Teacher.* Washington, D.C.: American Association of University Professors, 1971.

Educational Testing Service. *Comparative Data Guide—Student Instructional Report.* Princeton, N.J.: Educational Testing Service, 1975.

Educational Testing Service. *Comparative Data Guide for Two-Year Colleges and Technical Institutions—Student Instructional Report.* Princeton, N.J.: Educational Testing Service, 1977.

Edwards, S. A., and McCarrey, M. W. "Measuring the Performance of Researchers." *Research Management*, 1973, *16* (1), 34-41.

Elliot, D. H. "Characteristics and Relationships of Various Criteria of College and University Teaching." *Purdue University Studies in Higher Education*, 1950, *70*, 5-61.

Elmore, P. B., and LaPointe, K. A. "Effect of Teacher Sex, Student Sex, and Teacher Warmth on the Evaluation of College Instructors." *Journal of Educational Psychology*, 1975, *67*, 368-374.

Feldman, K. A. "Consistency and Variability Among College Students in Rating Their Teachers and Courses: A Review and Analysis." *Research in Higher Education*, 1977, *6* (3), 233.

Fenker, R. M. "The Evaluation of University Faculty and Administrators: A Case Study." *Journal of Higher Education*, 1975, *46*, 665-686.

Fentress, J. H., and Swanson, R. A. "The Effect of Instructor Influential Tactics on Their Evaluation by University Students." Unpublished master's thesis, Bowling Green State University, 1973.

Ferber, M. A., and Huber, J. A. "Sex of Student and Instructor: A Study of Student Bias." *American Journal of Sociology*, 1975, *80*, 949-963.

Festinger, L. *A Theory of Cognitive Dissonance.* Stanford, Calif.: Stanford University Press, 1957.

Fletcher, A., and Clark, J. L. D. "Performance Assessment." In R. R.

Reilly (Ed.), *Expert Assessment of Experiential Learning—A CAEL Handbook.* Columbia, Md.: Cooperative Assessment of Experiential Learning, 1977.

French-Lazovik, G. *Evaluation of College Teaching.* Washington, D.C.: Association of American Colleges, n.d.

Fuller, F. F., and Manning, B. A. "Self-Confrontation Reviewed: A Conceptualization for Video Playback in Teacher Education." *Review of Educational Research,* 1973, *43* (4), 469–528.

Furst, E. J. *Constructing Evaluation Instruments.* New York: Longmans, Green, 1958.

Gaff, J. G. *Toward Faculty Renewal: Advances in Faculty, Instructional, and Organizational Development.* San Francisco: Jossey-Bass, 1975.

Gilmore, G. M., Kane, M. T., and Naccarato, R. W. "The Generalizability of Student Ratings of Instruction: Estimation of Teacher and Course Components." *Journal of Educational Measurement,* 1978, *15* (1), 1–13.

Grasha, A. F. *Assessing and Developing Faculty Performance: Principles and Models.* Cincinnati, Ohio: Communication and Education Associates, 1977.

Grites, T. J. "Student Perceptions and Self-Perceptions of Faculty Members in the Related Roles of Classroom Teacher and Academic Advisor." Unpublished doctoral dissertation, University of Maryland, 1974.

Gronlund, N. E. *Constructing Achievement Tests.* Englewood Cliffs, N.J.: Prentice-Hall, 1968.

Gronlund, N. E. *Stating Behavioral Objectives for Classroom Instruction.* Toronto, Canada: Collier-Macmillan, 1970.

Guthrie, E. R. *The Evaluation of Teaching: A Progress Report.* Seattle: University of Washington Press, 1954.

Haberman, M., and Quinn, L. "Assessing Faculty's Community Service." *Adult Leadership,* 1977, *25,* 140–150.

Heider, F. *The Psychology of Interpersonal Relationships.* New York: Wiley, 1958.

Highet, G. "The Need to Make it New." *The Chronicle of Higher Education,* July 21, 1976, p. 40.

Hildebrand, M., Wilson, R. C., and Dienst, E. R. *Evaluating University Teaching.* Berkeley: Center for Research and Development in Higher Education, University of California, 1971.

Hodgson, T. F. *The General and Primary Factors in Student Evaluation of Teaching Ability.* Seattle: University of Washington Press, 1958.

Hollander, E. P. "The Friendship Factor in Peer Nominations." *Personnel Psychology,* 1956, *9,* 435–447.

Holmes, D. S. "Effects of Grades and Disconfirmed Grade Expectancies on Students' Evaluations of Their Instructor." *Journal of Educational Psychology,* 1972, *63,* 130–133.

Hoyt, D. P. "Background on the Uses and Misuses of Peer Evaluation—Perspectives from Another Campus." Unpublished manuscript, Iowa City, Iowa, 1977.

Hoyt, D. P., and Howard, G. S. "The Evaluation of Faculty Development Programs." *Research in Higher Education,* 1978, *8,* 25–38.

Ingle, R. B., and DeAmico, G. "The Effect of Physical Conditions of the Test Room on Standardized Achievement Test Scores." *Journal of Educational Measurement,* 1969, *6* (4), 237–240.

Isaacson, R. L., and others. "The Dimensions of Student Evaluations of Teaching." Ann Arbor: University of Michigan, 1964. (Mimeograph.)

Kaplin, W. A. *The Law of Higher Education: Legal Implications of Administrative Decision Making.* San Francisco: Jossey-Bass, 1978.

Kerlinger, F. "Student Evaluation of University Professors." *School and Society,* October 1971, pp. 353–356.

Kindsvatter, R., and Wilen, W. W. "Improving Classroom Instruction: A Self- and Shared-Analysis Approach." In. S. C. Scholl and S. C. Inglis (Eds.), *Teaching in Higher Education.* Columbus: Ohio Board of Regents, 1977.

Knapp, J., and Sharon, A. *A Compendium of Assessment Techniques.* Princeton, N.J.: Cooperative Assessment of Experiential Learning, 1975.

Kramer, H. C., and Gardner, R. E. *Advising by Faculty.* Washington, D.C.: National Education Association, 1977.

Krathwohl, D. R., and Payne, D. A. "Defining and Assessing Educational Objectives." In R. L. Thorndike (Ed.), *Educational Measurement.* (2nd. ed.) Washington, D.C.: American Council on Education, 1971.

Kulik, J. A., and McKeachie, W. J. "The Evaluation of Teachers in Higher Education." In F. N. Kerlinger (Ed.), *Review of Research in Education.* Vol. 3. Itaska, Ill.: Peacock, 1975.

Ladd, E. C., and Lipset, S. M. "Scholarly Articles Published by Professors." *The Chronicle of Higher Education,* November 28, 1977, p. 2.

Larson, R. L. *The Evaluation of Teaching College English.* New York: Modern Language Association of America and ERIC Clearinghouse on the Teaching of English in Higher Education, 1970.

Leventhal, L. "Teacher Rating Forms: Critique and Reformulation of Previous Validation Designs." *Canadian Psychological Review,* 1975, *16,* 269–276.

Leventhal, L., Perry, P., and Abrami, P. C. "Effects of Lecturer Quality and Student Perception of Lecturer's Experience on Teacher Ratings and Student Achievement." *Journal of Educational Psychology,* 1977, *69* (4), 360–374.

Lindvall, C. M. (Ed.). *Defining Educational Objectives.* Pittsburgh: University of Pittsburgh Press, 1964.

Linn, R. L., and Slinde, J. A. "The Determination of the Significance of Change Between Pre- and Posttesting Periods." *Review of Educational Research,* 1977, *47* (1), 121–150.

McCarthy, M. B. "Continuing Education Service as a Component of Faculty Evaluation." Paper presented at the Adult Education Research Conference, San Antonio, Texas, 1978.

McIntyre, C. "Evaluation of College Teachers." *Criteria,* No. 6, May 1977. [Ann Arbor: Center for Research on Learning and Teaching, University of Michigan.]

McKeachie, W. J., Lin, Y., and Mann, W. "Student Ratings of Teacher Effectiveness: Validity Studies." *American Educational Research Journal,* 1971, *8,* 435–445.

Madaus, G. F., Woods, E. M., and Nuttall, R. L. "A Causal Model Analysis of Bloom's Taxonomy." *American Educational Research Journal,* 1973, *10* (4), 253–262.

Mager, R. F. *Preparing Instructional Objectives.* Belmont, Calif.: Fearon, 1962.

Mager, R. F. *Measuring Instructional Intent.* Belmont, Calif.: Fearon, 1973.

Markham, R. "Influences of Handwriting Quality on Teacher Evaluation of Written Work." *American Educational Research Journal,* 1976, *13* (4), 277–283.

Marsh, H. W., Overall, J. U., and Kesler, S. P. "The Validity of Students' Evaluations of Instructional Effectiveness: A Comparison

of Faculty Self-Evaluations and Evaluations by Their Students."
Paper presented at the annual meeting of the Association of Institutional Research, San Diego, May 1978.

Marshall, J. C, and Powers, J. M. "Writing Neatness, Composition
Errors, and Essay Grades." *Journal of Educational Measurement*,
1969, *6* (2), 97–101.

Marso, R. N. "Test Item Arrangement, Testing Time, and Performance." *Journal of Educational Measurement*, 1970, *7* (2), 113–118.

Maslow, A. H ., and Zimmerman, W. "College Teaching Ability,
Scholarly Activity, and Personality." *Journal of Educational Psychology*, 1956, *47*, 185–189.

Mayhew, L. B. *Colleges Today and Tomorrow*. San Francisco:
Jossey-Bass, 1969.

Meltzer, L. "Scientific Productivity in Organizational Settings."
Journal of Social Issues, 1956, *12* (3), 32–40.

Menard, H. W. *Science: Growth and Change*. Cambridge, Mass.:
Harvard University Press, 1971.

Miller, R. I. *Evaluating Faculty Performance*. San Francisco: Jossey-
Bass, 1972.

Moomaw, W. E. "Practices and Problems in Evaluating Instruction."
In J. A. Centra (Ed.), *New Directions for Higher Education: Re-
newing and Evaluating Teaching*, no. 17. San Francisco: Jossey-
Bass, 1977.

Morsh, J. E., Burgess, G. G., and Smith, P. N. "Student Achievement
as a Measure of Instructor Effectiveness." *Journal of Educational
Psychology*, 1956, *47*, 79–88.

Morsh, J. E., and Wilder, E. S. "Identifying the Effective Instructor.
A Review of the Quantitative Studies, 1900–1952." ERIC Document
044371. Chanute, Ill.: Air Force Personnel and Training Research
Center, 1954.

Murray, H. G. "The Validity of Student Ratings of Teaching Ability."
Paper presented at the Canadian Psychological Association Meeting, Montreal, 1972.

Naftulin, D. H., Ware, J. E., and Donnelly, F. A. "The Doctor Fox
Lecture: A Paradigm of Educational Seduction." *Journal of
Medical Education*, 1973, *48*, 630–635.

New York Times. "On Evaluating Good Teaching." Letter to the
Editor, December 20, 1977.

Nitzsche, J. C. "How to Save Your Career." *Change*, 1978, *10* (2),
40–43.

O'Banion, T., Fordyce, J. W., and Goodwin, F. "Academic Advising in the Two-Year College: A National Survey." *Journal of College Student Personnel,* 1972, *13,* 411–419.

Olson, L. A. "A Third-Generation Student Instructional Rating System (SIRS)." Paper presented at the Association for Institutional Research Conference, Montreal, 1977.

O'Neil, J. M., and others. *Faculty and Staff Resources at the University of Kansas.* Lawrence, Kans.: University Counseling Center, 1978.

Overall, J. U., and Marsh, H. W. "Long-Term Stability of Students' Evaluation of Instruction: A Longitudinal Study." Paper presented at the Association for Institutional Research Conference, Houston, 1978.

Parent, E. R., Vaughan, C. E., and Wharton, K. "A New Approach to Course Evaluation." *Journal of Higher Education,* 1971, *42,* 113–118.

Parsons, T., and Platt, G. M. *The American Academic Professions: A Pilot Study.* Cambridge, Mass.: Harvard University Press, 1968.

Payne, D. A. *The Specification and Measurement of Learning Outcomes.* Waltham, Mass.: Blaisdell, 1968.

Perry, R. R., and Baumann, R. R. "Criteria for Evaluation of College Teaching: Their Reliability and Validity at the University of Toledo." In A. L. Sockloff (Ed.), *Proceedings: Faculty Effectiveness as Evaluated by Students.* Philadelphia, Pa.: Temple University, 1973.

Programs of Continuing Education. *Handbook of Legal Issues in Teacher Evaluation.* Princeton, N.J.: Information Division, Educational Testing Service, 1978.

Rodin, M., and Rodin, B. "Student Evaluations of Teachers." *Science,* 1972, *177,* 1164–1166.

Rose, C. "Stalking the Perfect Teacher." *The Chronicle of Higher Education,* October 4, 1976, p. 24.

Ryskamp, K. L., and Simon, A. M. "The First Amendment Freedoms of Speech, Press, and Association." In D. H. Blumer (Ed.), *Legal Issues for Postsecondary Education, Briefing Papers.* Washington, D.C.: American Association of Community and Junior Colleges, 1975.

Salomon, G., and McDonald, F. J. "Pretest and Posttest Reactions to Self-Viewing One's Teaching Performance on Video Tape." *Journal of Educational Psychology,* 1970, *61,* 280–286.

Sax, G., and Cromack, T. R. "The Effects of Various Forms of Item Arrangements on Test Performance." *Journal of Educational Measurement*, 1966, *3*, 309–311.

Scannell, D. P., and Tracy, D. B. *Testing and Measurement in the Classroom*. Boston: Houghton Mifflin, 1975.

Schrader, W. B. *Admissions Test Scores as Predictors of Career Achievement in Psychology*. GREB No. 76–1R. Princeton, N.J.: Educational Testing Service, 1978.

Scriven, M. "Value vs. Merit." *Evaluation News*, December 1978, No. 8, pp. 1–3.

Selden, D. "Faculty Bargaining and Merit Pay: Can They Co-Exist?" Point of View, *The Chronicle of Higher Education*, October 30, 1978, p. 72.

Seldin, P. "Survey of Current Faculty Evaluation Procedures." Report presented at the 4th International Conference on Improving University Teaching sponsored by University of Maryland, 1978.

Shur, G. M., and LeBlanc, R. P. "Legal Liability of Faculty." In D. H. Blumer (Ed.), *Legal Issues for Postsecondary Education*. Washington, D.C.: American Association of Community and Junior Colleges, 1975.

Smith, A. S. *Faculty Development and Evaluation in Higher Education*. Washington, D.C.: ERIC Higher Education Research Report, No. 8, 1976.

Soloff, S. "Effect of Non-Content Factors on the Grading of Essays." *Graduate Research in Education and Related Disciplines*, 1973, *6*, 44–54.

Southern Regional Education Board. *Faculty Evaluation for Improved Learning*. Atlanta: Southern Regional Education Board, 1977.

Spencer, R. E. *The Course Evaluation Questionnaire: Manual of Interpretation*. Urbana: Office of Institutional Research, University of Illinois, 1965.

Stallings, W. M., and Singhal, S. "Some Observations on the Relationships Between Research Productivity and Student Evaluation of Courses and Teaching." Paper presented at the American Educational Research Association Conference, Los Angeles, 1969.

Stanley, J. C., and Hopkins, K. D. *Educational and Psychological Measurement and Evaluation*. Englewood Cliffs, N.J.: Prentice-Hall, 1972.

Stecklein, J. E. "Approaches to Measuring Workload Over the Past Two Decades." In J. I. Doi (Ed.), *New Directions for Higher Education: Assessing Faculty Effort*, no. 2. San Francisco: Jossey-Bass, 1974.

Stone, E. F., Rabinowitz, S., and Spool, M.D. "Effect of Anonymity on Student Evaluations of Faculty Performance." *Journal of Educational Psychology*, 1977, *69* (3), 274–280.

Stone, E. F., Spool, M. D., and Rabinowitz, S. "Effects of Anonymity and Retaliatory Potential on Student Evaluations of Faculty Performance." *Research in Higher Education*, 1977, *6*, 313–325.

Sullivan, A. M., and Skanes, G. R. "Validity of Student Evaluation of Teaching and the Characteristics of Successful Instructors." *Journal of Educational Psychology*, 1974, *66*, 584–590.

Swanson, R. A., and Sisson, D. J. "The Development, Evaluation, and Utilization of a Department Faculty Appraisal System." *Journal of Industrial Education*, 1971, *9* (1), 64–79.

Sweeney, J. M., and Grasha, A. F. "Improving Teaching Through Faculty Development Triads." *Improving College and University Teaching Yearbook*. Corvallis: Oregon State University Press, 1978.

Thorne, G. L. "Student Ratings of Instructors: From Scores to Administrative Decisions." *Journal of Higher Education*, in press.

Thorne, G. L., Scott, C. S., and Beaird, J. H. *Assessing Faculty Performance*. Monmouth: Teaching Research Division, Oregon State System of Higher Education, 1976.

Tuckman, B. W., and Oliver, W. F. "Effectiveness of Feedback to Teachers as a Function of Source." *Journal of Educational Psychology*, 1968, *59*, 297–301.

Turnbull, W. W. "Testing Scores in Perspective." *Educational Record*, 1978, *59* (4), 291–296.

Voeks, V. W. "Publications and Teaching Effectiveness." *Journal of Higher Education*, 1962, *33*, 212.

Webb, W. B., and Nolan, C. Y. "Student, Supervisor, and Self-Ratings of Instructional Proficiency." *Journal of Educational Psychology*, 1955, *46*, 42–46.

Weeks, M. L. "A Teacher Learns What Really Counts." *The Chronicle of Higher Education*, July 5, 1977, pp. 3–4.

Wilson, D., and Doyle, K. O., Jr. "Student Ratings of Instruction: Student and Instructor Sex Interactions." *Journal of Higher Education*, 1976, *47* (4), 465.

Winer, B. J. *Statistical Principles in Experimental Design*. New York: McGraw-Hill, 1962.

Wood, P. H. "Student and Peer Ratings of College Teaching and Peer Ratings of Research and Service: Four Years of Departmental Evaluation." Bowling Green, Ohio: Bowling Green State University, n.d. (Mimeograph.)

Wotruba, T. R., and Wright, P. L. "How to Develop a Teacher-Rating Instrument: A Research Approach." *Journal of Higher Education*, 1975, *46* (6), 653–663.

Yonge, G. D., and Sassenrath, J. M. "Student Personality Correlates of Teacher Ratings." *Journal of Educational Psychology*, 1968, *59*, 44–52.

Index